The 2023 Ultimate
MEDITERRANEAN
DIET COOKBOOK
For Beginners

Enjoy 2000 Days of Simple, Delicious, and Budget-Friendly Recipes to
Embrace Healthy Living. Includes a Stress-Free 84-Day Meal Plan

ARIA
Tennyson

GET YOUR BONUS

The digital version of "PLANT BASED COOKBOOK" is 100% FREE.
You don't need to enter any details except
your name and email address.

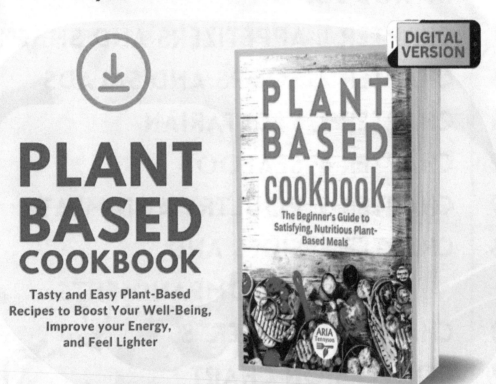

PLANT BASED COOKBOOK

Tasty and Easy Plant-Based
Recipes to Boost Your Well-Being,
Improve your Energy,
and Feel Lighter

TO DOWNLOAD YOUR BONUS SCAN THE QR CODE BELOW OR GO TO

http://bonusforbooks.com/aria-tennyson-md

SCAN ME

TABLE OF CONTENTS

INTRODUCTION

Introduction

Mediterranean diet is a diet style which is based on the eating habits of Mediterranean people in Greece and Southern Italy. The diet is characterized by high intake of vegetables, fruits, breads, fish and olive oil; moderate consumption of dairy products and red wine; low intake of meat and poultry (and low to moderate intake of cheese); as well as reduced sugar/sweeteners/junk foods.

Since then, we found that this diet not only keeps us lean but also helps us live longer once we get old. The diet helps strengthen our brain, protect us against heart attacks, strokes and even cancer.

The diet is considered a beneficial eating plan among many scientists and nutritionists. According to a study conducted at Harvard, the Mediterranean Diet can help lessen the risk of heart disease and cancer by up to 70 percent. The Mediterranean Diet also helps lower the chances of suffering from diabetes by up to 50 percent and keeps you from putting on weight.

There are several other studies which have shown that the Mediterranean Diet helps people live a healthier life, so there is no wonder that thousands of Americans follow it. The benefit-packed diet is also considered to be one of the most balanced eating plans in the world. According to nutritionists, the Mediterranean Diet helps ward off inflammation, which helps keep your brain working at its best and prevents depression. The cardiovascular system and blood arteries also benefit from this. And it wards off pain and discomfort in your bowels and digestive tract.

This diet style is practically perfect because it helps control weight gain by keeping you full longer than any other kind like low-carb diets or no-carb diets. Since it is also rich in fiber content, this diet style helps maintain your heart and digestive health.

Highly nutritious Mediterranean Diet is made up of ingredients like vegetables, fruits, fish and nuts. It also includes indulgences like cheese and red wine. And you can have fresh vegetables and fruits during the summer season which are very rich in phytonutrients. It is a kind of diet that promises you good health as well as fulfillment of all your nutritional needs. The Mediterranean Diet can help you live a fuller life, free from diseases and illnesses. And this diet style also helps you avoid unnecessary medications.

This diet style is so versatile that you can adapt it according to your preference. And you can also include some other elements of a healthy lifestyle, like exercise and proper sleep. This is because this diet style focuses on eating healthy food, which gives out much more benefits than just losing weight or being a healthier person.

Research reveals that this diet helps the body to burn fat at a faster rate. So, if you want to lose weight with no special efforts on your part, try this natural, powerful weight loss program. The Mediterranean Diet helps us keep our weight at a level which will keep us healthy and fit.

With the help of this diet, we can take care of our health by doing right eating habits. And this diet style also helps you live longer. The Mediterranean Diet is a way to help you overcome illnesses and diseases that can weaken your immune system and lead to other health problems like heart attacks, strokes, diabetes, cancer etc.

It has been a long time since we have lived in the Mediterranean Region. But after learning about the benefits of this healthy lifestyle, we realized that much more could be learned from it than from foods from other regions. With this diet, we can also live a happier, healthier life which is full of fun and happiness.

Studies show that the Mediterranean Diet is not only very healthy for adults but also for kids. It has been found that most kids don't eat many vegetables or fruit and are obese because of junk foods and refined sugar. But with proper Mediterranean Diet, including the right amount of calories, the right kinds of fat, protein and carbs as well as vegetables and fruits - kids will lead healthy lives without much effort.

There are other benefits like helping your child sleep better at night by eating less junk food before bedtime. This diet style helps with emotional stability by giving them more control over their mood swings. And kids with the Mediterranean Diet style will have better grades in school and will also have better social skills than the ones who don't.

If you are a parent and want your child to grow healthy and strong, this diet style is perfect for you. It can help your child learn healthy eating habits from a young age and help them maintain their weight. The Mediterranean Diet is very efficient in reducing risk of diseases like diabetes, heart disease or cancer. The diet also helps boost brain power by getting rid of toxins that can cause damage to the mind. There are also many people who follow the Mediterranean Diet style, and it has helped them live longer.

The diet helps keep you full for longer than any other food plan. And it also helps in preventing depression and balancing mood swings. Stress levels are controlled by the Mediterranean Diet, which makes it easier for us to handle problems in our daily lives, like exams or job interviews. In addition, this diet will keep your stress levels low and won't make you feel hungry. There are many benefits of following this diet style that can be noticed just by changing your eating habits.

It is the best diet if you are looking to shed pounds quickly. The diet is designed by a nutritionist and is very easy to follow. It has no recipes which can make it frustrating for beginners. This diet style helps you lose weight fast without counting calories or calorie intake. Many people who have tried the Mediterranean Diet style have noticed that the weight loss is gradual and steady, instead of sudden and quick.

Main Differences with Other Diets

The Mediterranean diet is a lot like some diets and extremely different from others, and we're going to take a quick look at these similarities and differences.

DASH diet

Out of all the diets we will talk about, this one is the most similar to the Mediterranean diet. It was designed by professionals to prevent and treat cardiovascular and hypertense patients to help them diminish the risk of heart disease and stroke. Like the Mediterranean diet, DASH also gives you complete creative freedom when it comes to the meals and foods you cook and eat, as long as you follow its guidelines. They are also alike in their lack of restrictions; all they do is strongly advise against the consumption of certain foods.

In fact, the foundations on which DASH was built on are almost the same as those for the Mediterranean diet. For example, the consumption of fruits and vegetables is strongly emphasized. Legumes and healthy fats are also encouraged.

Both diets also turn away from red meats, processed grains, added sugars, and excess salt. Perhaps where they differ slightly is with the preferred type of animal protein and the amount of salt. DASH allows for poultry as much as fish, while the Mediterranean diet strongly favors fish and seafood over everything else.

The daily intake of salt is also extremely controlled under DASH, unlike the Mediterranean diet. Other than that, we can say they are more similar than alike.

Keto diet

The ketogenic diet was actually developed for patients suffering from epilepsy, not cardiovascular disease. In a nutshell, it is high in fat, low in carbohydrates, and recommends moderate consumption of animal protein. Thus, the principles behind the keto diet are the opposite of those for the Mediterranean diet.

In short, the keto diet promotes a hearty consumption of cheese and other dairy products, oils, red meats, and low-carb vegetables. This is exactly what the Mediterranean diet hopes to keep you away from. Not to mention that whole grain or not, all carbohydrates are off the table in the keto diet, unlike with the Mediterranean diet. The keto diet is also strongly associated with quick weight loss, whereas the Mediterranean diet isn't.

Paleo diet

This is considered a weight loss diet that promotes the consumption of fruits and vegetables, as well as fish. However, carbohydrates, legumes, and dairy products are completely off the table on the paleo diet because the whole point is to eat as simplistically as possible, like in the days of hunter-gatherers.

While the Mediterranean diet discourages the consumption of dairy products, it does encourage the consumption of all kinds of carbohydrates as long as they are whole-grain, and legumes, too. The paleo diet is also restrictive, which the Mediterranean diet is not.

One thing they both have in common, though, is that they both try to cut out processed foods as much as possible. Actually, the Mediterranean diet leaves some room for exploration since it is not restrictive, but for the paleo diet anything that has been processed is a huge NO.

Atkins diet

Out of all the diets we have mentioned, the Atkins one is the absolute complete opposite of the Mediterranean diet. The Atkins diet was designed for weight loss, and it is extremely high in fats and very low in carbohydrates. This diet is like the keto diet on steroids because, while it is also high-fat and low-carb, the Atkins diet has almost complete disregard for the consumption of fruits and vegetables. Without needing to explain much more, the Mediterranean diet is already the opposite of the Atkins diet.

The Atkins diet also encourages the consumption of all kinds of processed foods as long as they are high in calories and fat, and low in carbs. That means cheeses, sodas, salad dressings, beef, pork, bacon, ice cream - all of these foods are allowed under this diet. For this reason, we believe it is needless to explain why the Mediterranean diet is so unlike it. Everything you are encouraged to eat on the Atkins diet is exactly what you should be avoiding in the Mediterranean diet; they are almost exact opposites.

Health Benefits of The Mediterranean Diet:

The Mediterranean diet gained popularity in the medical field because of its documented benefits to heart health. But, plenty of research has shown that this regime can have a much longer list of health benefits that go beyond the heart. Below some details:

Heart Health and Reduced Risk of Stroke

Heart health is greatly impacted by diet. Maintaining healthy levels of good cholesterol, blood sugar, blood pressure and staying within proper weight results in optimal heart health. What you eat affects directly each of these components.

People who are most at risk are often advised to start eating a low-fat diet. Such a diet seeks to reduce all fats, including those from oils, nuts and red meat.

This is because the unsaturated fats consumed in the Mediterranean diet lower bad cholesterol levels while also increasing good cholesterol levels. Cholesterol is a compound having a place with the sterol or steroid liquor subgroup of natural atoms.

It is delegated a waxy steroid of fat. It is a basic segment of cell layers and an antecedent to the creation of fat-solvent nutrients, for example, nutrient D.

There are two primary kinds of cholesterol HDL (high-thickness lipoproteins) and LDL (low-thickness lipoproteins). Despite the fact that this isn't completely precise, HDL and LDL are lipoproteins. They are the vehicle components for cholesterol particles. They are made out of proteins and fats.

LDL particles transport cholesterols from the liver to the cells of the body.

HDLs absorbs any cholesterol found in the tissues or created by different organs and conveys it back to the liver for reprocessing.

This is the reason HDLs are, in some cases alluded to as "good" cholesterol since they get any that are dropped in the circulation system before they can stick to the organs. LDL is known as "bad" cholesterol.

A lot of cholesterol in the circulation system may build an individual's danger of coronary illness, for the most part, atherosclerosis. This is the reason balance in HDL/LDL particles is so significant, and lopsidedness can be perilous.

Feature on Trans-Fats

Trans-fats are recorded as hydrogenated or incompletely hydrogenated oils. The oils might be soy, canola or any partly hydrogenated "vegetable" oil. This is the most worst form of fat you can ingest.

As indicated by the Mayo Clinic, trans-fats raise LDL levels and bring down HDL levels.

It is a man-made fat found in prepared merchandise and other bundled nourishments. Notwithstanding causing HDL/LDL irregularity, it raises complete blood triglycerides (fats that typically take course in the circulation system) and advance plaque development on blood vessel dividers.

Another significant part of the Mediterranean eating regimen is greasy fish.

This incorporates lake trout, salmon, sardines, herring, mackerel, and apoundacore fish. They have a lot of omega-3 unsaturated fats.

This sort of unsaturated fat assists with diminishing blood coagulating and brings down triglyceride levels. High triglyceride levels (in excess of 150 mg) can cause heart illnesses. Omega-3 unsaturated fats are likewise connected with assisting with directing circulatory strain, decline the danger of unexpected coronary episode, and improve the general strength of our veins.

Significant Features of a Mediterranean Diet:

1. The essential wellspring of fat in this eating routine is olive oil.
2. Dinner regularly incorporates a glass of red wine.
3. Vegetables and occasional new organic products are a significant piece of each dinner.
4. Whole grain pasta and bread are served with no kind of conciliatory sentiment.
5. Meat is consumed in small portions, and red meat is essentially kept away.
6. Popular flavors incorporate garlic, basil, oregano, lemon, rosemary, and mint.

The Mediterranean diet also highlights the importance of daily activity and stress reduction by enjoying quality time with people you love. While eating more plant-based foods, each of these elements significantly reduces the risk of many heart-related conditions and improves heart health. By increasing your intake of vegetables and fresh fruits while adding in regular daily activities, you improve not just your heart health but overall health.

Reduces Age-Related Muscle and Bone Weakness

Eating a well-balanced diet that provides you with a wide range of vitamins and minerals is essential for reducing muscle weakness and bone degradation. This is especially important as you age. Accident-related injuries such as tripping, falling or slipping while walking can cause serious injury. As you age, this becomes even more of a concern as some simple falls can be fatal. Many accidents occur because of weakening muscle mass and the loss of bone density. Women, especially those who are entering the menopause phase of their life, are at a greater risk of serious injury from accidental falls because the estrogen levels decline significantly at this time. This decrease in estrogen results in a loss of bone and muscle mass.

The decrease of estrogen can also cause bone thinning, which over time develops into osteoporosis.

Maintaining healthy bone mass and muscle agility as you age can be challenging. When you are not getting the proper nutrients to promote healthy bones and muscles, you increase your risk of developing osteoporosis.

The Mediterranean diet offers you a simple way to fulfill the dietary needs necessary to improve bone and muscle functioning.

Antioxidants, vitamins C and K, carotenoids, magnesium, potassium, and phytoestrogens are essential minerals and nutrients for optimal musculoskeletal health.

Plant-based foods, unsaturated fats, and whole grains help provide you with the necessary balance of nutrients that keep your bones and muscles healthy. Sticking with a Mediterranean diet can improve and reduce the loss of bone mass as you age.

Reduces the Risk of Alzheimer's

Alzheimer's is a common brain disorder in older adults, 60 years of age or older, but the first signs of Alzheimer's can be present in adults as young as 50 years old.

Those with Alzheimer's suffer from: disorientation, memory loss, inability to think clearly, speech problems, impaired judgment, visual and spatial disorientation.

The condition can progress fast or slowly depending on how quickly the neurons in the brain begin to die off. Though the decline begins in the hippocampus area of the brain it becomes widespread as it progresses.

Individuals with Alzheimer's show a significant increase in beta-amyloid proteins in the brain and have a much lower level of brain energy. Research has focused on trying to identify those who are at greater risk of dementia early on through brain scans and imaging. In one such study, brain scans were conducted on 70 individuals between the ages of 30 and 60 at the beginning of the study and then two years later. The scans showed that those on the Western diet had significant loss in brain energy levels and an increase in the beta-amyloid build-up as opposed to those on the Mediterranean diet [Mediterranean Diet May Slow Development, 2018].

This indicates that diet can have an impact on the leading two significant causes of the development of Alzheimer's disease. Just as diet can impact other areas of your health, it can affect your brain health as well. Cholesterol, blood sugar, and blood vessel health can contribute to your risk of developing Alzheimer's disease.

The best sources of fuel for the brain are fresh fruits vegetables that supply it with vital vitamins and nutrients. When processed foods, refined grains, and added sugars are consumed too often, this impairs the brain's functionality as these foods release toxins into the body.
These toxins then cause widespread inflammation and the brain begins to build up plaque, which causes a malfunction to cognitive ability [Nutrition and Dementia, 2019].

The Western diet consists of a number of foods that increase the risk of Alzheimer's disease, such as processed meat, refined grains like white bread and pasta, and added sugar. Foods that contain diacetyl, which is a chemical commonly used in the refinement process, increase beta-amyloid plaque build-up in the brain. Microwaveable popcorn, margarine, and butter are some of the most consumed foods that contain this harmful chemical. It is no wonder that Alzheimer's is becoming one of the leading causes of death among Americans.
The Mediterranean diet, instead, includes a wide range of foods that have been proven to boost memory and slow down cognitive decline. Dark leafy vegetables, fresh berries, extra virgin olive oil, and fresh fish contain brain-boosting vitamins and minerals that can improve brain health. The Mediterranean diet can help you make the necessary diet and lifestyle changes that can greatly decrease your risk of Alzheimer's.

Reduces Risk of Parkinson's Disease
Research has shown progress in the treatment of Parkinson's, but many therapies today are still based on medications and therapies that only help individuals manage symptoms, not slow or stop the progress of the disease. Genetics and environmental factors have been researched to better understand what causes the development of Parkinson's disease. While genetics plays a factor, exposure to pesticides, herbicides, high cholesterol, low vitamin D levels, and limited physical activity can all increase the risk of Parkinson's disease.

Those with Parkinson's disease will suffer from: tremors, muscle stiffness, balance troubles, difficulty walking, depression, sleep problems and cognitive disruptions.

Parkinson disease is also common among individuals who have a higher level of oxidative stress. This damage the cell in the brain and can result in serious cognitive and physical decline.

The Mediterranean diet encourages the consumption of antioxidant-rich foods such as fresh fruits and vegetables. Eating organic and locally grown fruits and vegetables reduces the risk of toxin exposure from pesticides and herbicides.

Those with Parkinson's are often encouraged to change their diet so that it includes more healthy fats, like extra virgin olive oil, seeds, and nuts, fresh fruits, organic vegetables, and whole grains. This diet recommendation is the basis of the Mediterranean diet. Individuals are also encouraged to reduce the consumption of salt, sugar, and empty-calorie foods, which is also what the Mediterranean diet encourages.

Protects Against Type 2 Diabetes

The Mediterranean diet is the most recommended diet from health professionals for those diagnosed with Type 2 diabetes or prediabetes. Healthy foods and regular exercise that the Mediterranean diet promotes are two of the key components to help individuals manage and even see a remission of symptoms.

When the body stops responding normally to insulin, a condition known as type 2 diabetes sets established. The result is a hazardous increase in blood sugar. Your blood sugar or glucose is what gives your body energy. It supplies fuel to your muscles, tissues, and cells so they are able to function properly. A build-up of glucose in your body can cause a long list of health complications. The body may turn to use its own muscle and fat to get the energy it needs. Blood vessels can also become damaged, which increases the risk of heart attack and stroke.

Those who are at the greatest risk of developing Type 2 diabetes include: individuals who are overweight or obese, individuals who have limited physical activity, people with family history of Type 2 diabetes and individuals who have insulin resistance.

The most common symptoms of Type 2 diabetes include: excessive fatigue, frequent numbness of the hands or feet, tingling feelings in the hands and feet, regular headaches, vision difficulties, increase in urination, unquenchable thirst.

Many individuals are unaware of their condition until a serious health complication arises because of the condition. Those with Type 2 diabetes are at a greater risk of heart attack, stroke, organ damage, loss of vision, hearing loss, and many other health conditions that can decrease quality of life and shorten your lifespan.

What you eat contributes to the production of insulin and how efficiently your body is able to use the insulin produced. Carbohydrates are converted to glucose for the body to use as energy. Many individuals are eating too many unhealthy carbs, causing the body to be thrown out of balance and blood sugar levels to rise and remain at an elevated level. The most common foods known to spike glucose levels are white bread, pasta, and sugary beverages. The excessive sugar and simple carbs found in these items cause the body to have a sudden increase in glucose which the body often cannot handle fast enough.

Carbohydrates themselves are not all bad, and when you choose the right ones, they can help slow down the release of glucose, making it easier for the body to absorb the energy. Complex carbs, which are found naturally in many fruits, vegetables, and whole grains, get slowly released into the bloodstream. Eating foods high in fiber also helps slow down the release of glucose.

Type 2 diabetes has been strongly connected with diet. Diets high in trans-fat, sugar, simple carbohydrates, and sodium increase the risk of developing diabetes. People who transition to a Mediterranean diet lower their risk of Type 2 diabetes. Those who have been diagnosed with pre-diabetes, which is often a red flag diagnosis that almost always leads to a diagnosis of Type 2 diabetes, can reverse the diagnosis. Those who suffer from diabetes will often find that the Mediterranean diet can help them significantly reduce symptoms and take control of their insulin and blood sugar levels. The Mediterranean diet encourages improvement in both diet and physical activity, both important aspects in the treatment of diabetes.

How to Adopt a Mediterranean Diet:

Vegetables Should Be the Primary Course.

The Mediterranean diet is plant-based, and you should eat veggies at every meal; some studies recommend at least three to five servings per day. The Mediterranean Diet recommends consuming a range of colorful vegetables as the core component of this eating plan. Vitamins, minerals, fiber, and antioxidant phytochemicals found in vegetable aid in lowering inflammation and deliver a nutritious and illness-fighting boost.

The following vegetables are often used in the Mediterranean diet: Artichokes, arugula, beets, broccoli, Brussels sprouts, cabbage, carrots, celery, celeriac, chicory, collard greens, cucumbers, dandelion greens, eggplant, fennel, kale, leeks, lemons, lettuce, Mache, mushrooms, mustard greens, nettles, okra, onions (red, sweet, white), peas, peppers, potatoes, pumpkin, and purslane.

Use Extra Virgin Olive Oil

One of the most noticeable aspects of the Mediterranean diet is that olive oil is one of its main components. It is considered a healthy fat with several advantages, including heart health, blood pressure control, and weight management. Due to its particular flavor and scent, it is a fun element in every Mediterranean dish. There aren't any Mediterranean recipes that don't use this item. Extra virgin olive oil is tasty, healthful, and well worth the money, whether you use it as a dip, dressing, or drizzle. As a result, it is one of the foods you should consume in more enormous proportions.

Concentrate on Whole Grain Foods

The Mediterranean diet does not include processed foods. Choose meals such as bulgur or oats with just one to three whole-food components—rice, whole-wheat flour, oats, and whole-wheat pasta, rich in vitamins and minerals. Whole foods are fruits, vegetables, whole grains, nuts, legumes, seafood, and extra virgin olive oil are whole foods.

Eat Fresh Fruit

Fresh fruit is another component of the Mediterranean diet, and studies recommend three servings per day. Fruit, like vegetables, is high in antioxidants, fiber, vitamins, and minerals.

Fruits including apples, apricots, avocados, cherries, clementines, dates, figs, grapes, melon, nectarine, olives, oranges, peaches, pears, pomegranates, strawberries, tangerines, and tomatoes are common in the Mediterranean diet.

Dairy products should be eaten in moderation.

A conventional Mediterranean diet could contain a few portions of cheese or yogurt each week for dairy. Substitute savory cheeses like Parmesan, feta, or part-skim mozzarella for processed American slices, and go for plain Greek yogurt over flavored varieties if you're watching your sugar intake.

Enjoy Vegan Recipes

The majority of your meals should include veggies, and studies have shown that even 2-4 vegetable servings per day may lower the risk of cardiovascular disease. Add spinach to your eggs, pile your sandwich high with avocado and cucumber, and eat an apple with nut butter instead of crackers to gradually increase your vegetable intake.

Choose Skim Milk

Pick skim milk, consume natural yogurt, and white cheeses like ricotta or cottage cheese to follow the Mediterranean Diet and lose weight. Always choose skim or low-fat varieties. If you need to sweeten natural yogurt, a spoonful of honey or jam will be enough.

Eat Fish and Seafood 3 Times Every Week

Fish and seafood should be eaten at least three times a week because they are high in protein and good fats like omega-3. These natural anti-inflammatories may aid joint discomfort, blood circulation, and heart disease prevention.

Red meat should be avoided whenever possible.

According to research published in the British Medical Journal, consuming red meat, mainly processed types, is linked to an increased risk of early death. That's why red meat should be restricted to once a week; try other meals with beneficial protein sources like eggs, fish, and whole-grain foods like rice and beans, and you should also include rice and lentils or rice and peas.

Ingredients and Pantry Staples

Even though we have talked about what foods you should be eating on the diet, it's time to get into the little details and put a face to the names. Like we've mentioned, the Mediterranean diet is all about eating simple, wholesome foods. After all, we hardly believe that Ancient Greece had specialty supermarkets where you could find hundreds of imported alternatives for the same product. The higher class was also extremely small in size compared to the rest of the population, which means the Mediterranean diet was more of a middle-class eating pattern than an exclusively higher class one.

Having said this, we are going to be sticking to simple staples for the most part. Nevertheless, this does not mean that you cannot enjoy more complex meals or try out recipes with new ingredients if that's what you are into. All we are trying to say is that the Mediterranean diet is intrinsically simple, and you don't need to complicate it unless you want to.

For the most part, we will be working with ingredients that are local to the Mediterranean. It's important to note that the meals you will be preparing will mostly be low in sodium too, but just as delicious because they also emphasize the use of spices and herbs in order to flavor their food.

Even if you are not into cooking that much, you will be surprised at what some garlic, parsley, basil, and paprika can do. Despite this, the general food groups you should be consuming are universes of their own, and we are going to help you break down exactly what each of these should consist of in order to make your culinary journey a lot smoother and your trips to the supermarket much shorter.

Examples of fish and seafood:

Salmon

Tuna (fresh, not canned)

Mackerel

Sardines

Tilapia

Eel

Sea bass

Shrimp

Squid

Octopus

Oysters

Mussels

Crab

Clam

While fresh is always best, we won't get picky if the only seafood you can get a hold of is frozen. However, make sure it is not breaded, spiced, or prepared in any sort of way. See to ensure that it sounds as natural as possible.

Examples of whole grains:

Oatmeal

Brown rice

Whole grain pasta

Millet

Couscous

Bulger

Barley

Whole grain bread

Barley

Buckwheat

Examples of healthy fats:

Olive oil

Flaxseed oil

Soybean oil

Examples of nuts and seeds:

Almonds

Walnuts

Hazelnuts

Macadamias

Peanuts

Cashews

Pine nuts

Pistachios

Sunflower seeds

Chia seeds

Flaxseed

When buying nuts and seeds, make sure to get the unsalted versions.

Examples of fruits:

Dates

Figs

Apricots

Apples

Grapes

Melon

Pomegranate

Peaches

Clementine

Examples of vegetables:

Tomatoes

Zucchinis

Portobello mushrooms

Eggplant

Carrots

Red onions

Bell peppers

Examples of legumes:

Cannellini beans

Chickpeas

Lentils

Kidney beans

When it comes to legumes, there are a lot of options on the market - especially canned varieties. We're not going to say no to canned legumes completely, but we will suggest using them in moderation or for last-minute meals when you're too tired to cook.

The secret is to rinse and drain them extremely well so you can remove all of the sodium and salt from the solution they were in. Nonetheless, we will say that it's always better to get the raw versions whenever possible, and just let them soak overnight. Not only is it better and it will yield more servings, but it is also significantly cheaper than buying canned legumes every time.

Examples of herbs and spices:

Parsley

Mint

Basil

Thyme

Paprika

Garlic

Cumin

Fennel

Dill

Rosemary

Fresh garlic is always the tastiest, but when it comes to other herbs and spices, we won't be so picky. Get them fresh or ground, whichever you will get the most use out of. In our opinion, ground spices are better. Even though it is true that they lose their taste after a while, we find them way more convenient than fresh herbs and spices which tend to go bad very quickly.

Thus, unless you're making homemade basil pesto, dried and ground herbs and spices might be your best bet too.

Cooking Techniques and Tools

Mediterranean-style cooking is known for its simple yet flavorful dishes that often utilize fresh ingredients and traditional cooking techniques. Here are some of the cooking techniques and tools commonly used in Mediterranean-style cooking:

1. Grilling: Grilling is a popular cooking technique in Mediterranean-style cooking, especially for seafood and vegetables. Grilling enhances the natural flavors of the ingredients and adds a smoky flavor. Grilled meats such as lamb or chicken are often marinated in herbs, spices, and olive oil to enhance the flavor.

2. Roasting: Roasting is another common cooking technique in Mediterranean-style cooking, especially for meats and vegetables. Roasting enhances the natural sweetness of the ingredients and adds a caramelized flavor. Roasted vegetables such as eggplant, peppers, and tomatoes are often used in Mediterranean-style dips such as baba ghanoush or muhammara.

3. Using a mortar and pestle: A mortar and pestle is a traditional tool used in Mediterranean-style cooking to grind herbs, spices, and garlic into a paste. This technique is commonly used to make traditional dishes such as pesto, hummus, and tzatziki.

4. Clay pots and tagines: Clay pots and tagines are traditional cookware used in Mediterranean-style cooking. Clay pots are used to slow-cook stews and soups, while tagines are used to cook meats and vegetables with spices and herbs. These cookware types retain moisture and flavor, resulting in tender and flavorful dishes.

When selecting and using Mediterranean-style cookware, it's essential to choose high-quality materials that can withstand high temperatures and retain moisture. Here are some tips:

1. Choose high-quality clay pots and tagines made from unglazed terra-cotta or ceramic materials that are safe for oven and stovetop use.

2. Soak clay pots and tagines in water for at least 30 minutes before use to prevent cracking or breakage due to thermal shock.

3. Use a heat diffuser when cooking with clay pots and tagines to prevent direct contact with the heat source, which can cause the pot to crack or break.

Mediterranean-style cooking is known for its simple yet flavorful dishes that often utilize fresh ingredients and traditional cooking techniques.

Grilling, roasting, using a mortar and pestle, and cooking with clay pots and tagines are just a few of the many techniques and tools used in Mediterranean-style cooking.

When selecting and using Mediterranean-style cookware, it's essential to choose high-quality materials that can withstand high temperatures and retain moisture.

CHAPTER 1
APPETIZERS AND SNACKS

1. Cream Cheese & Tomato Toast

Preparation time: five mins
Cooking time: zero mins
Servings: four
Ingredients:

• one tomato, cubed

12 oz. cream cheese, soft

¼ cup mayonnaise

two garlic cloves, crushed

one red onion, sliced

two tbsps. lime juice

4 slices whole-wheat toast

Directions:

1. Inside a container, blend cream cheese, mayonnaise, garlic, onion, and lime juice until smooth.
2. Spread the compote onto the bread slices and top with the tomato cubes to serve.

Per serving: Calories: 210kcal; Fat: 7g; Carbs: 8g; Protein: 5g

2. Almond Spinach with Chickpeas

Preparation time: 5 minutes
Cooking time: 0 minutes
Servings: 4
Ingredients:

2 tbsp olive oil

3 spring onions, chopped

1 cup baby spinach

15 oz canned chickpeas, drained

Salt and black pepper to taste

2 tbsp lemon juice

1 tbsp cilantro, chopped

2 tbsp almonds flakes, toasted

Directions:

1. Toss chickpeas, spring onions, spinach, salt, pepper, olive oil, lemon juice, and cilantro inside a container.
2. Serve topped with almond flakes.

Per serving: Calories: 230kcal; Fat: 6g; Carbs: 10g; Protein: 16g

3. Jalapeno Poppers Stuffed with Hummus

Preparation time: one hr + chilling time
Cooking time: 50 mins
Servings: six
Ingredients:

½ lb. chickpeas, soaked overnight

1 lb. jalapeño peppers, seeded and halved

1 shallot

2 tbsp tahini

1 tbsp lemon juice

3 tbsp olive oil

½ tsp red pepper flakes

1 tsp cumin

1 tsp harissa seasoning

1 garlic clove, minced

Salt to taste

1 tbsp paprika

Directions:

1. Preheat oven to 400F. Pour the chickpeas in a pot over medium heat and cover with water by 1 inch. Bring to a boil, after lower and simmer for 45-50 minutes. Remove 1 cup of the cooking liquid to a bowl and drain the chickpeas. Reserve some whole chickpeas for garnishing.
2. Bake the jalapeño peppers in the preheated oven for ten mins. Eliminate to a serving platter. Pour the chickpeas in a food processor and half of the reserved cooking liquid and pulse until no large pieces remain. Add the remaining cooking liquid, lemon juice, olive oil, red pepper flakes, cumin, harissa seasoning, garlic, tahini, shallot, and salt.
3. Pulse until smooth. Spoon the hummus into each jalapeño pepper half and top with the whole chickpeas.
4. Lastly, add paprika before serving.

Per serving: Calories: 250kcal; Fat: 12.7g; Carbs: 27.9g; Protein: 8.9g

4. Thyme Artichoke with Aioli

Preparation time: 25 minutes
Cooking time: 10 minutes
Servings: 4
Ingredients:

1 tbsp olive oil

1 red onion, chopped

2 garlic cloves, minced

Salt and black pepper to taste

10 oz canned artichoke hearts, drained

one teaspoon lemon juice

one cup light mayonnaise

2 tbsp thyme, chopped

Directions:

1. Warm the cooking oil in a pan over lower-medium heat and cook the onion for 3 minutes.
2. Stir in artichokes, salt, and pepper and stir-fry for four to four mins; reserve. Inside a container, combine mayonnaise, lemon juice, and garlic.
3. Sprinkle the artichokes with thyme and offer using aioli.

Per serving: Calories: 120kcal; Fat: 8g; Carbs: 7g; Protein: 3g

5. Red Pepper and Fresh Mozzarella

Preparation time: twenty mins
Cooking time: 0 mins
Servings: four
Ingredients:

one bowl of fresh mozzarella

quarter cup of quality olive oil

1/4 cup basil leaves, julienned

1 large red pepper

Salt and pepper to taste
Directions:

1. Mix ingredients and relish!

Per serving: Calories: 166kcal; Fat: 13g; Carbs: 9g; Protein: 6g

6. Parmesan Sandwiches

Preparation time: 25 minutes
Cooking time: 20 minutes
Servings: 2
Ingredients:

1/2 cup all-purpose flour

1 large egg lightly beaten

3/4 cup of breadcrumbs

3 tablespoons grated parmesan cheese

2 skinless and boneless chicken breast halves (5 ounces each)

1/8 teaspoon salt

1/8 teaspoon pepper

2 tablespoons of olive oil

2 Italian bread rolls, divided

2 slices of provolone cheese

1/3 cup of marinara sauce or other meatless pasta sauce, heated
Directions:

1. Separate the flour and egg into two separate shallow bowls. Mix the breadcrumbs in another bowl with parmesan cheese.
2. Pound the chicken with ½-in. wooden hammer thickness. Sprinkle with salt and pepper.
3. Put the chicken in the flour to cover both sides; shake off the excess. Dip the egg into the crumb mixture.

21

4. Heat the oil in a 9-inch frying skillet over high heat. Add the chicken; Bake until the chicken is golden and no longer pink, 4 to 5 minutes per side.

5. Serve in sandwiches with provolone cheese and sauce.

Per serving: Calories: 669kcal; Fat: 32g; Carbs: 45g; Protein: 48g

7. Cheese & Cucumber Mini Sandwiches

Preparation time: five mins
Cooking time: 0 mins
Servings: four
Ingredients:

four bread slices

one cucumber, cut

2 tbsp cream cheese, soft

1 tbsp chives, chopped

¼ cup hummus

Salt and black pepper to taste

Directions:

1. In a bowl, mix hummus, cream cheese, chives, salt, and pepper until combined.

2. Spread the mixture onto bread slices.

3. Top with cucumber and cut each sandwich into three pieces.

4. Serve instantly.

Per serving: Calories: 190kcal; Fat: 13g; Carbs: 5g; Protein: 9g

8. Garbanzo Patties with Yogurt Sauce

Preparation time: 20 mins
Cooking time: twenty mins
Servings: four
Ingredients:

three garlic cloves, minced

one cup canned garbanzo beans, drained

two tbsps. parsley, sliced

one onion, sliced

1 teaspoon ground coriander

Salt and black pepper, as required

quarter teaspoon cayenne pepper

quarter teaspoon cumin powder

1 teaspoon lemon juice

3 tbsp flour

¼ cup olive oil

¼ cup Greek yogurt

2 tbsp chopped cilantro

½ tsp garlic powder

Directions:

1. In a blender, blitz garbanzo, parsley, onion, garlic, salt, pepper, cayenne pepper, cumin powder, and lemon juice until smooth.

2. Remove to a bowl and mix in flour. Form 16 balls out of the mixture and flatten them into patties. Warm the cooking oil in a pan over lower-medium heat and fry patties for 10 minutes on both sides.

3. Remove to a place a double sheet of kitchen paper to drain the excess fat. Inside a container, combine the Greek yogurt, cilantro, garlic powder, salt, and pepper.

4. Serve the patties with yogurt sauce.

Per serving: Calories: 120kcal; Fat: 8g; Carbs: 14g; Protein: 4g

9. Grilled Eggplant Rounds

Preparation time: 25 minutes
Cooking time: 20 minutes
Servings: 4
Ingredients:

4 tbsp olive oil

2 eggplants, cut into rounds

1 cup roasted peppers, chopped

½ cup Kalamata olives, chopped

one teaspoon red chili flakes, crumpled

Salt and black pepper, as required

2 tbsps. basil, chopped

two tbsp Parmesan cheese, grated

Directions:

1. Combine roasted peppers, half of the olive oil, olives, red chili flakes, salt, and pepper in a bowl. Rub each eggplant slice with remaining olive oil and salt grill them on the preheated grill for 14 minutes on both sides.
2. Remove to a platter. Distribute the pepper mixture across the eggplant rounds and top with basil and Parmesan cheese to serve.

Per serving: Calories: 220kcal; Fat: 11g; Carbs: 16g; Protein: 6g

10. Double Tomato Bruschetta

Preparation time: 15 mins
Cooking time: 20 mins
Servings: 8
Ingredients:

6 Roma tomatoes, chopped

½ cup of sun-dried tomatoes in oil

3 cloves of chopped garlic

1/4 cup of olive oil

1/4 cup fresh basil, stems removed

2 tablespoons balsamic vinegar

1/4 teaspoon salt

1/4 teaspoon ground black pepper

1 French baguette

2 cups of grated mozzarella cheese

Directions:

1. Preheat the oven to the grill setting.
2. In a large bowl, toss together the tomatoes (both fresh and sun-dried), the garlic, olive oil, vinegar, basil, salt, and pepper. Let the mixture stand for 10 minutes.

3. Cut the baguette into 1-inch slices. Place the baguettes on a pan in a single layer. Lightly brown them on the grill for a minute or two.
4. Spread the tomato mixture evenly over the baguettes. Cover with the mozzarella cheese slices.
5. Grill for 5 minutes or until cheese is melted.

Per serving: Calories: 215kcal; Fat: 8.9g; Carbs: 24.8g; Protein: 9.6g

11. Garlic Lentil-Walnut Spread with Cilantro

Preparation time: 40 minutes
Cooking time: 55 minutes
Servings: 6
Ingredients:

1 cup split red lentils

½ red onion

1 garlic bulb, top removed

½ tsp cumin seeds

1 tsp coriander seeds

1 roasted red bell pepper, chopped

4 tbsps. olive oil

quarter cup walnuts

two tbsp tomato paste

½ tsp Cayenne powder

Salt and black pepper to taste

2 tbsp fresh cilantro, chopped

Directions:

1. Preheat the oven to 370 F. Drizzle the garlic with half of the olive oil and wrap it in a aluminum foil. Roast for 35-40 minutes. Let it cool for ten mins.
2. Cover the lentils with salted water in a pot over medium heat and bring to a boil. Lower and simmer for 17 minutes. Drain and set aside.
3. Smash the garlic and place them in a food processor.
4. Add cooled lentils, cumin seeds, coriander seeds, roasted red bell pepper, onion, walnuts, tomato paste, Cayenne powder,

rest of the olive oil, salt, and black pepper. Pulse till uniform.

5. Top with cilantro and serve with crostini or crackers.

Per serving: Calories: 234kcal; Fat: 12.78g; Carbs: 21.7g; Protein: 9.9g

12. Artichoke & Bean Spread

Preparation time: ten mins
Cooking time: ten mins
Servings: four
Ingredients:

two tbsps. olive oil

15 oz can Cannellini beans, drained

1 red onion, chopped

6 oz canned artichoke hearts, drained

4 garlic cloves, minced

1 tbsp thyme, chopped

½ lemon, juiced and zested

Salt and black pepper to taste

Directions:

1. Onion and garlic should be sautéed in oil over low to medium heat for about five minutes, or until the onion becomes translucent. Add the artichoke hearts and cook for 2-3 more minutes.

2. Set aside to cool slightly. Transfer the cooled mixture to a blender along with cannellini beans, thyme, lemon juice, lemon zest, pepper and salt. Blitz until it becomes smooth.

3. Serve.

Per serving: Calories: 280kcal; Fat: 12g; Carbs: 19g; Protein: 17g

13. Roasted Pepper Hummus

Preparation time: 10 minutes
Cooking time: 0 minutes
Servings: 6
Ingredients:

4 tbsp olive oil

6 oz roasted red peppers, chopped

16 oz canned chickpeas, drained

¼ cup mayonnaise

3 tbsp tahini paste

1 lemon, juiced

3 garlic cloves, minced

Salt and black pepper to taste

1 tbsp parsley, chopped

Directions:

1. In a blender, pulse red peppers, chickpeas, mayonnaise, tahini paste, lemon juice, garlic, salt, and pepper until you obtain a smooth mixture.

2. Continue blending while gradually adding olive oil until smooth.

3. Serve sprinkled with parsley.

Per serving: Calories: 260kcal; Fat: 12g; Carbs: 18g; Protein: 7g

14. Almond & Parmesan Stuffed Cucumbers

Preparation time: 10 minutes
Cooking time: 0 minutes

24

Servings: 4

Ingredients:

3 cucumbers, julienned and deseeded

¼ tsp salt

1 garlic clove, minced

2 tbsp dill, chopped

¼ cup aggravated Parmesan cheese

quarter cup almonds, sliced

quarter cup olive oil

½ tsp paprika

Directions:

1. Season cucumbers and arrange on a platter. Mix dill, almonds, garlic, Parmesan cheese, and olive oil in a food processor until smooth. Spoon the pesto sauce over the cucumbers and season with paprika to serve.

Per serving: Calories: 182kcal; Fat: 16g; Carbs: 10g; Protein: 4g

---

15. Cheesy Grilled Asparagus

Preparation time: 25 mins

Cooking time: ten mins

Servings: four

Ingredients:

two tbsps. olive oil

one lb. asparagus, trimmed

4 tbsp Grana Padano cheese, grated

½ teaspoon garlic powder

Salt, as required

two tbsps. parsley, sliced

Directions:

1. Preheat the grill to high. Season the asparagus with salt and garlic powder and coat with olive oil.

2. Grill the asparagus for 10 minutes, occasionally turning until lightly charred and tender.

3. Pour to a serving platter and sprinkle with cheese and parsley.

Per serving: Calories: 105kcal; Fat: 8.6g; Carbs: 4.7g; Protein: 4.3g

CHAPTER 2
SOUPS AND SALADS

16. Greek Avocado Salad

Preparation time: 10 mins
Cooking time: zero mins
Servings: 8
Ingredients:

two English cucumbers, cut

one and a half lbs. tomatoes, chopped

¼ red onion, sliced

½ cup Kalamata olives, sliced

¼ cup fresh parsley, chopped

2 avocados, peeled, cored, and sliced

one cup feta cheese, crumbled

½ cup additional-virgin olive oil

half cup red wine vinegar

2 garlic cloves, minced

1 tablespoon dried oregano

two teaspoons sugar

one teaspoon kosher salt

one teaspoon ground black pepper

Directions:

1. Inside a big serving container, combine the tomatoes, parsley, onions, cucumbers, avocado, and olives. Serve immediately. Put away.
2. Inside a jar, mix together the vinegar, sugar, olive oil, salt, oregano, and garlic along with the pepper. Put the top back on and give it a good whisk to get the solution mixed.
3. To customise the flavour to your liking, try seasoning it with some freshly ground black pepper, sugar, and salt. Now that the dressing is ready...
4. Place the dressing in the salad container and mix everything together thoroughly. Serve.

Per serving: Calories: 360kcal; Fat: 32.5g; Carbs: 16.2g; Protein: 5.6g

17. Carrot Salad with Lemon Vinaigrette

Preparation time: 15 mins
Cooking time: 0 mins
Servings: four
Ingredients:

1 lb. peeled carrots

2 tsp Dijon mustard

1 tbsp freshly squeezed lemon juice, from one lemon

1-1/2 tbsp vegetable oil

1-1/2 tbsps. additional virgin olive oil

one to two tsp honey to taste

quarter tsp salt

1/4 tsp freshly ground to taste black pepper

2 tbsp chopped fresh parsley

2 finely sliced scallions

1 tbsp finely chopped shallots

Directions:

1. In a food processor, grate the carrots. Just set aside.
2. Mix the Dijon mustard, lemon juice, honey, vegetable oil, olive oil, salt and pepper in a salad bowl. Add the carrots, scallions (or shallots) and fresh parsley and toss well. If necessary, taste and adjust the seasoning.
3. Cover till prepared to serve, and refrigerate.

Per serving: Calories: 222kcal; Fat: 0.6g; Carbs: 58.2g; Protein: 1.3g

18. Italian Cavolo Nero Soup

Preparation time: ten mins
Cooking time: 25 mins
Servings: four
Ingredients:

two tbsp olive oil

one lb. cavolo Nero, torn

1 cup canned chickpeas, drained

Salt and black pepper to taste

1 celery stalk, chopped

1 onion, chopped

1 carrot, chopped

14 oz canned tomatoes, chopped

2 tbsp rosemary, chopped

4 cups vegetable stock

Directions:

1. Warm the olive oil in medium-skillet over medium heat and cook onion, celery, and carrot for 5 minutes.
2. Stir in cavolo Nero, salt, pepper, tomatoes, rosemary, chickpeas, and vegetable stock and simmer for twenty mins.
3. Serve warm.

Per serving: Calories: 200kcal; Fat: 9g; Carbs: 13g; Protein: 5g

---

19. Minestrone Soup

Preparation time: 10 minutes
Cooking time: thirty mins
Servings: six
Ingredients:

two tablespoons olive oil

one-third cup parmesan cheese, shredded

2 shredded garlic cloves, shredded

1 onion, sliced

3 celery stalks, sliced

1/3-pound green beans, chopped

1 carrot, diced

1 teaspoon dried oregano

Salt and black pepper, to taste

1 teaspoon dried basil

14 ounces crumpled tomatoes

twenty-eight ounces crushed tomatoes

2 cups chicken stock

one cup elbow pasta

fifteen ounces kidney beans

two tablespoons fresh basil, sliced

Directions:

1. Five mins should be spent frying the onions in warmed up olive oil across a moderate flame setting. After stirring it in, sauté the garlic for a further thirty seconds. After incorporating the carrot and celery, continue cooking for an additional five mins while mixing regularly.
2. After adding the oregano, green beans, salt, basil, and black pepper, continue to mix frequently while cooking for another three mins.
3. After adding the tomatoes and the broth, allow the mixture to come to a simmer. Turn the heat down to low and keep it at that for the next ten mins. Cook for an additional ten mins after adding the pasta and kidney beans to the pot.
4. Include some salt and serve.

Per serving: Calories: 260kcal; Fat: 8g; Carbs: 37g; Protein: 15g

---

20. Italian Sausage & Seafood Soup

Preparation time: 15 minutes
Cooking time: 30 minutes
Servings: 4
Ingredients:

½ lb. shrimp, raw and deveined

2 tbsp butter

3 Italian sausages, sliced

1 red onion, chopped

1 ½ cups clams

one carrot, sliced

one celery stalk, sliced

two garlic cloves, crushed

one (fourteen and a half ounces) canned tomatoes

one teaspoon dried basil

1 teaspoon dried dill

4 cups chicken broth

2 tbsp olive oil

4 tbsp corn flour

2 tbsp lemon juice

2 tbsp fresh cilantro, chopped

Salt and black pepper to taste

Directions:

1. Pour the butter in a pot over medium heat and brown the sausage; set aside. Warm the olive oil in the same pan and add in corn flour; cook for 4 mins.
2. Include in the onion, garlic, carrot, and celery and stir-fry them for 3 minutes. Stir in tomatoes, basil, dill, and chicken broth. Raise to a simmer.
3. After, lower the flame and simmer for 5 mins. Mix in the reserved sausages, salt, black pepper, clams, and shrimp and simmer for 10 mins.
4. Discard any unopened clams. Share into bowls and sprinkle with lemon juice.
5. Serve warm garnished with fresh cilantro.

Per serving: Calories: 619kcal; Fat: 42.6g; Carbs: 26.6g; Protein: 32.5g

21. Mediterranean Cobb Salad

Preparation time: 15 mins
Cooking time: 10 mins
Servings: four
Ingredients:

4 cups of fresh baby spinach leaves

4 cups of spring romaine mix lettuce

6 bacon slices, cooked to the crisp and crumbled finish

3 hard diced boiled eggs

2 diced Roma tomatoes

1 avocado, peeled, pit removed, and diced

three-quarter cup of crumbled feta cheese

half cup black thinly sliced olives

For the Dressing:

1/2 cup of yogurt

2 tbsp milk, or use lemon juice, olive oil, or water

1 clove finely minced garlic

2 tsp fresh finely minced parsley

Salt and pepper to taste

Directions:

1. Spinach and lettuce should be mixed together in a big salad bowl before being topped with bacon, eggs, tomatoes, avocado, cheese, and olives.
2. Whisk the yogurt, milk, garlic, parsley, salt and pepper inside a separate mixing container.
3. Taste and adjust the dressing accordingly.
4. Whisk in a little more milk, lemon juice, or olive oil if you need to thin out the dressing.
5. Drizzle salad across the dressing and serve!

Per serving: Calories: 222kcal; Fat: 0.6g; Carbs: 58.2g; Protein: 1.3g

22. Spicy Lentil Soup

Preparation time: 15 minutes
Cooking time: 30 minutes
Servings: 4
Ingredients:

1 cup lentils, rinsed

1 onion, chopped

2 carrots, chopped

1 potato, cubed

1 tomato, chopped

4 garlic cloves, crushed

four cups vegetable broth

two tbsps. olive oil

½ tsp chili powder

Salt and black pepper to taste

2 tbsp fresh parsley, chopped

Directions:

1. Warm olive oil in a skillet over medium heat. Add in onion, garlic, and carrots and sauté for 5-6 minutes until tender. Mix in lentils, broth, salt, pepper, chili powder, potato, and tomato.
2. Bring to a boil, then, lower and simmer for 20 minutes, stirring often. Top with parsley and serve.

Per serving: Calories: 331kcal; Fat: 9g; Carbs: 44.3g; Protein: 19g

23. Veggie & Chicken Soup

Preparation time: 15 minutes
Cooking time: 20 minutes
Servings: 4
Ingredients:

1 cup mushrooms, sliced

2 tsps. olive oil

1 large carrot, sliced

1 yellow onion, chopped

one celery stalk, sliced

two yellow squash, sliced

two chicken breasts, cubed

½ cup chopped fresh parsley

4 cups chicken stock

Salt and black pepper to taste

Directions:

1. Warm the oil in a skillet over lower-medium heat. Place in carrot, onion, mushrooms, and celery and cook for five mins.

2. Mix in chicken and cook for 12 more mins. Mix in squash, salt, and black pepper.
3. Cook for 5 mins, afterwards lower the flame and pour in the stock. Cook covered for 10 more minutes. Divide between bowls and scatter with parsley.
4. Serve instantly.

Per serving: Calories: 335kcal; Fat: 9g; Carbs: 28g; Protein: 33g

24. Corn & Black Bean Salad

Preparation time: ten mins
Cooking time: 0 mins
Servings: 4
Ingredients:

two tbsps. vegetable oil

quarter cup balsamic vinegar

1/2 teaspoon of salt

1/2 teaspoon of white sugar

1/2 teaspoon ground cumin

1/2 teaspoon ground black pepper

1/2 teaspoon chili powder

3 tablespoons chopped fresh coriander

1 can beans, rinsed and drained

1 can of sweetened corn (8.75 oz) drained

Directions:

1. Combine balsamic vinegar, oil, salt, sugar, black pepper, cumin and chili powder in a small bowl.
2. Combine black corn and beans in a medium bowl. Mix with vinegar and oil vinaigrette and garnish with coriander. Cover and refrigerate overnight.

Per serving: Calories: 214kcal; Fat: 8.4g; Carbs: 28.6g; Protein: 7.5g

25. Pork Meatball Soup

Preparation time: fifteen mins
Cooking time: 30 mins
Servings: four
Ingredients:

two tbsp olive oil

½ cup white rice

½ lb. ground pork

Salt and black pepper to taste

2 garlic cloves, minced

1 onion, chopped

½ tsp dried thyme

4 cups beef stock

½ tsp saffron powder

14 oz canned tomatoes, crushed

1 tbsp parsley, chopped

Directions:

1. In a bowl, mix ground pork, rice, salt, and pepper using your hands. Form the solution into ½-inch balls; put aside. Warm the olive oil in a pot over medium heat and cook the onion and garlic for 5 minutes. Pour in beef stock, thyme, saffron powder, and tomatoes and bring to a boil.

2. Add in the pork balls and cook for 20 minutes. Adjust the seasoning with salt and pepper. Serve sprinkled with parsley.

Per serving: Calories: 380kcal; Fat: 18g; Carbs: 29g; Protein: 18g

26. Cucumber and Tomato Salad

Preparation time: ten mins
Cooking time: zero mins
Servings: four
Ingredients:

Salt and black pepper, to taste

1 tablespoon fresh lemon juice

1 onion, chopped

1 cucumber, peeled and diced

2 tomatoes, chopped

4 cups spinach

Directions:

1. In a salad bowl, mix the onions, cucumbers, and tomatoes. Season with pepper and salt to taste.

2. Add the lemon juice and mix well. Add the spinach, toss to coat, serve and relish.

Per serving: Calories: 70.3kcal; Fat: 0.3g; Carbs: 8.9g; Protein: 2.2g

27. Leftover Lamb & Mushroom Soup

Preparation time: 5 minutes
Cooking time: 25 minutes
Servings: 4
Ingredients:

2 carrots, chopped

1 red onion, chopped

2 tbsp olive oil

2 celery stalks, sliced

two garlic cloves, crushed

Salt and black pepper, as required

1 tbsp thyme, chopped

4 cups vegetable stock

1 cup white mushrooms, sliced

8 oz leftover lamb, shredded

14 oz canned chickpeas, drained

2 tbsp cilantro, chopped

Directions:

1. Warm the olive oil in medium skillet over medium heat and cook onion, celery, mushrooms, carrots, and thyme for 5 minutes until tender. Stir in vegetable stock and lamb and bring to a boil. Lower heat and simmer for 20 minutes.

2. Mix in chickpeas and cook for an additional 5 minutes. Ladle your soup into individual bowls.

3. Top with cilantro and serve hot.

Per serving: Calories: 300kcal; Fat: 12g; Carbs: 23g; Protein: 15g

28. Lamb & Spinach Soup

Preparation time: fifteen mins
Cooking time: 40 mins
Servings: four
Ingredients:

two tbsp olive oil

½ lb. lamb meat, cubed

3 eggs, whisked

4 cups beef broth

5 spring onions, sliced

two tbsps. mint, sliced

2 lemons, juiced

Salt and black pepper, as required

one cup baby spinach

Directions:

1. Warm the olive oil in a mid-size pan over medium heat and cook lamb for 10 minutes, stirring occasionally. Add in onions and cook for another 4 minutes.
2. Pour in beef broth, salt, and pepper and simmer for 30 mins. Whisk eggs with lemon juice and some soup and pour into the pot along with the spinach and cook for 5 minutes.
3. Sprinkle with mint and serve immediately.

Per serving: Calories: 290kcal; Fat: 29g; Carbs: 3g; Protein: 6g

29. German Hot Potato Salad

Preparation time: ten mins
Cooking time: thirty mins
Servings: 12
Ingredients:

9 peeled potatoes

6 slices of bacon

1/8 teaspoon ground black pepper

1/2 teaspoon celery seed

2 tablespoons white sugar

2 teaspoons salt

3/4 cup water

1/3 cup distilled white vinegar

2 tablespoons all-purpose flour

3/4 cup chopped onions

Directions:

1. Bring an enormous pot of salted water to a boil. Toss in the potatoes and cook for 30 minutes, or until tender but holding their shape. Drain, let cool and cut finely.
2. Cook the bacon in a pan over lower-medium heat. Drain, crumble and set aside. Save the cooking juices.
3. Fry onions in bacon grease until golden brown.
4. Combine flour, sugar, salt, celery seed, and pepper in a small bowl. Add sautéed onions and cook, stirring until bubbling, and remove from heat. Stir in the water and vinegar, then bring back to the fire and bring to a boil, stirring constantly. Boil and stir. Slowly add bacon and potato slices to the vinegar/water mixture, stirring gently until the potatoes are warmed up.

Per serving: Calories: 205kcal; Fat: 6.5g; Carbs: 32.9g; Protein: 4.3g

30. Mediterranean Salad Recipe

Preparation time: 10 minutes
Cooking time: 0 minutes
Servings: 4
Ingredients:

4 cups of salad greens

2 medium tomatoes chopped

3 medium cucumber chopped

1/2 red or purple onion sliced

8 Oz. Feta cheese

Sundried Tomato Vinaigrette

Directions:

1. Place the salad greens, tomatoes, cucumber, onion, and feta cheese on a medium serving plate or in a medium bowl.

2. For self-serving, serve sundried tomato vinaigrette on the side.

Per serving: Calories: 221kcal; Fat: 13g; Carbs: 17g; Protein: 12g

CHAPTER 3
VEGETARIAN

31. Loaded Portobello Mushrooms

Preparation time: ten mins
Cooking time: 45 mins
Servings: four
Ingredients:

4 portobello mushrooms, stems removed

two cups arugula

¼ cup chopped fresh basil leaves

2 tbsp olive oil

1 onion, finely chopped

1 zucchini, chopped

¼ tsp dried thyme

⅛ tsp red pepper flakes

2 garlic cloves, minced

½ cup grated Parmesan cheese

Salt and black pepper to taste

Directions:

1. Preheat oven to 350F. Heat olive oil inside a nonstick pan across moderate flame and fry onion, arugula, zucchini, thyme, salt, pepper, and red flakes for 5 mins. Mix in garlic and sauté for 1 minute. Turn the heat off.
2. Mix in basil and scoop into the mushroom caps and arrange them on a baking sheet.
3. Top with Parmesan cheese and bake for 30-40 minutes, until mushrooms are nice and soft and cheese is dissolved.

Per serving: Calories: 128kcal; Fat: 8g; Carbs: 5.9g; Protein: 3g

32. Cauliflower Curry

Preparation time: 10 minutes
Cooking time: twenty-five mins
Servings: four
Ingredients:

two tablespoons olive oil

½ cauliflower, sliced into florets

¼ teaspoon salt

1 teaspoon curry paste

1 cup coconut milk

quarter cup fresh cilantro, chopped

1 tablespoon lime juice

Directions:

1. Cauliflower should be cooked for ten mins in olive oil that has been warmed up across moderate flame. Cauliflower should be simmered for ten mins after the coconut milk and curry powder have been combined, then added to the cauliflower.
2. After adding the lime juice and cilantro, mix everything together thoroughly. Serve, and have fun with it!

Per serving: Calories: 243kcal; Fat: 24g; Carbs: 9g; Protein: 3g

33. Greek-Style Potatoes

Preparation time: 10 mins
Cooking time: 1 hour 30 mins
Servings: four
Ingredients:

one-third cup olive oil

2 garlic cloves, sliced

1½ cups water

Salt and black pepper, as required

quarter cup lemon juice

one teaspoon rosemary

one teaspoon thyme

1 chicken bouillon cubes

2 potatoes, sliced

Directions:

1. Arrange the potatoes in a single layer on a baking sheet. After thoroughly combining all of the components in a large dish, pour it across the potatoes.
2. Bake for one hour and ten mins in a microve that has been prepared to 350 degrees Fahrenheit. Serve, and have fun with it!

Per serving: Calories: 418kcal; Fat: 18.5g; Carbs: 58.6g; Protein: 7g

34. Eggplant, Arugula & Sweet Potato Mix

Preparation time: ten mins
Cooking time: fifteen mins
Servings: four
Ingredients:

four cups arugula

2 baby eggplants, diced

two sweet potatoes, diced

1 tablespoon olive oil

one red onion, cut into wedges

one tsp hot paprika

2 tsp cumin, ground

Salt and black pepper to taste

¼ cup lime juice

Directions:

1. Warm the olive oil in a medium-skillet over medium heat and cook eggplants and potatoes for 5 minutes.
2. Mix in onion, paprika, cumin, salt, pepper, and lime juice and cook for another 10 minutes.
3. Mix in arugula and serve.

Per serving: Calories: 210kcal; Fat: 9g; Carbs: 13g; Protein: 5g

35. Stuffed Bell Peppers

Preparation time: 10 minutes
Cooking time: 50 minutes
Servings: 4
Ingredients:

1 cup cooked brown rice

4 oz crumbled feta cheese

4 cups fresh baby spinach

3 Roma tomatoes, chopped

4 red bell peppers, tops and seeds removed

2 tbsp olive oil

1 onion, finely chopped

1 cup mushrooms, sliced

2 garlic cloves, minced

1 tsp dried oregano

Salt and black pepper to taste

2 tbsp fresh parsley, chopped

Directions:

1. Warm up microwave to 350F. Heat oil in a large skillet across moderate flame and fry onion garlic and mushrooms for 5 mins. Stir in tomatoes, spinach, rice, salt, oregano, parsley, and pepper, cook for 3 minutes until the spinach wilts. Remove from the heat. Fill the bell peppers with the rice and top with feta cheese.

2. Arrange the peppers on a greased baking pan and pour in 1/4 cup of water. Bake covered with aluminum foil for 30 min. Then, bake uncovered for another 10 minutes.

Per serving: Calories: 387kcal; Fat: 15.1g; Carbs: 55.1g; Protein: 11.5g

36. Simple Sautéed Cauliflower

Preparation time: 10 mins
Cooking time: fifteen mins
Servings: four
Ingredients:

1 onion, sliced

one head cauliflower

quarter cup olive oil

one cup cherry tomatoes

two tablespoons raisins

one teaspoon white sugar

1 garlic clove, crushed

1 teaspoon dried parsley

¼ teaspoon red pepper flakes

one tablespoon lemon juice

Directions:

1. Warm olive oil inside a griddle measuring ten inches in diameter over moderate flame. Toss in the onion and keep cooking until it's soft. (around five to ten mins are sufficient).

2. After the onion has been sautéed, stir in the cauliflower, cherry tomatoes, raisins, and white sugar. Approximately four to five mins, during which time the griddle should be covered and the cauliflower should be

stirred on a regular basis, cooking should be completed.

3. Combine the cauliflower with the minced garlic, chopped parsley, and some crushed red pepper flakes. Raise the temperature to its highest setting.

4. Sauté for 1–3 minutes until the cauliflower gets browned.

5. Sprinkle the juice of the lemon across the cauliflower.

Per serving: Calories: 196.5kcal; Fat: 13.9g; Carbs: 17.8g; Protein: 3.7g

37. Zucchini Noodles Marinara

Preparation time: 10 minutes
Cooking time: 25 minutes
Servings: 4
Ingredients:

16 oz zucchini noodles

1 (14-oz) can chopped tomatoes, drained

1 onion, chopped

4 garlic cloves, crushed

two (fourteen oz) tins chopped tomatoes

2 tbsp olive oil

1 tbsp dried Italian seasoning

one teaspoon dried oregano

Salt, as required

quarter teaspoon crushed red pepper flakes

¼ cup Romano cheese, grated

Directions:

1. Warm oil in a large pan over moderate heat and sauté onion and garlic for 5 minutes, frequently stirring, until fragrant. Pour in tomatoes, oregano, Italian seasoning, salt, and red pepper flakes.

2. Bringing to a simmer, diminish the flame, and low boil gently for 10-15 mins. Stir in the zucchini noodles and cook for 3-4 minutes until the noodles are slightly softened. Scatter with Romano cheese and serve.

Per serving: Calories: 209kcal; Fat: 8.9g; Carbs: 27.8g; Protein: 8.1g

38. Spiralized Carrot with Peas

Preparation time: 10 minutes
Cooking time: 10 minutes
Servings: 4
Ingredients:

4 carrots, spiralized into noodles

1 sweet onion, chopped

2 cups peas

two garlic cloves, crushed

two tbsps. olive oil

¼ cup sliced fresh parsley

Salt and black pepper to taste

Directions:

1. Heat 2 tbsp of olive oil in a pot over medium heat and sauté the onion and garlic for 3 minutes until just tender and fragrant. Add in spiralized carrots and cook for 4 minutes. Mix in peas, salt, and pepper and cook for 4 minutes.
2. Drizzle with the remaining olive oil then drizzle via parsley to serve.

Per serving: Calories: 157kcal; Fat: 7.3g; Carbs: 19.6g; Protein: 4.8g

39. Brussels Sprouts and Pistachios

Preparation time: 10 mins
Cooking time: 30 mins
Servings: four
Ingredients:

one lb. Brussels sprouts, halved lengthwise and trimmed

4 shallots, peeled and quartered

½ cup roasted pistachios, chopped

½ lemon, zested and juiced

¼ teaspoon fine sea salt

quarter tsp. black pepper

one tablespoon olive oil

Directions:

1. Warm up the microwave to 400 deg. F. Line a baking sheet with foil.

2. Inside a container, toss the shallots and Brussels sprouts in olive oil. Make sure the sprouts are well coated. Top with salt and pepper prior to spreading them onto the baking sheet.
3. Bake for 15 minutes. Your vegetables should be lightly caramelized as well as tender.
4. Take the tray out and toss the sprouts with the lemon zest, lemon juice, and pistachios. Serve and enjoy!

Per serving: Calories: 126kcal; Fat: 7g; Carbs: 14g; Protein: 6g

40. Catalan-Style Spinach

Preparation time: 10 minutes
Cooking time: 5 minutes
Servings: 4
Ingredients:

4 cups fresh baby spinach

1 garlic clove, minced

2 tbsp raisins, soaked

2 tbsp toasted pine nuts

2 tbsp olive oil

Salt and black pepper to taste

Directions:

1. Warm olive oil in a very large skillet over moderate heat and sauté spinach and garlic for 3 minutes until the spinach wilts. Mix in raisins, pine nuts, salt, and pepper and cook for 3 minutes. Serve immediately.

Per serving: Calories: 111kcal; Fat: 10g; Carbs: 5.5g; Protein: 1.8g

41. Garlic Kale with Almonds

Preparation time: 10 minutes
Cooking time: 15 minutes
Servings: 4
Ingredients:

¼ cup slivered almonds

1-pound chopped kale

¼ cup vegetable broth

1 lemon, juiced and zested

2 tbsp olive oil

1 garlic clove, minced

1 tbsp red pepper flakes

Salt and black pepper to taste

Directions:

1. Heat olive oil inside a griddle across moderate flame and fry kale, salt, and pepper for 8-9 mins until soft. Add lemon juice, lemon zest, red pepper flakes, and vegetable broth and continue cooking until the liquid evaporates, about 3-5 minutes. Garnish with almonds and serve.

Per serving: Calories: 123kcal; Fat: 8.1g; Carbs: 10.8g; Protein: 4g

42. Chili Artichokes with Carrots

Preparation time: 10 minutes
Cooking time: 35 minutes
Servings: 4
Ingredients:

10 frozen artichoke hearts, halved

1 onion, sliced

12 whole baby carrots

½ cup chopped celery

1 lemon, juiced

2 tbsp chopped fresh basil

1 red chili, sliced

2 tbsp olive oil

1 tbsp butter

¾ cup frozen fava beans

Salt and black pepper to taste

Directions:

1. Warm olive oil in a pot over moderate heat and sauté onion, carrots, and celery for 7-8 minutes until tender. Stir in lemon juice, butter and 1 cup of water.

2. Boil, lower the heat and simmer gently for 10-15 minutes. Add in artichoke hearts, fava beans, salt, and pepper and cook covered for another 10 minutes. Top with basil and serve.

Per serving: Calories: 353kcal; Fat: 4.1g; Carbs: 67.7g; Protein: 22.1g

43. Cheesy Eggplant Rolls

Preparation time: 10 minutes
Cooking time: 25 minutes
Servings: 4
Ingredients:

1 ½ cups ricotta cheese

2 (14-oz) cans crushed tomatoes

1 shallot, finely chopped

2 garlic cloves, minced

1 tbsp Italian seasoning

1 tsp dried oregano

2 eggplants

½ cup grated mozzarella cheese

two tbsps. olive oil

Salt, as required

¼ tsp red pepper flakes

Directions:

1. Warm up microwave to 350F. Heat olive oil in a skillet across moderate flame and fry shallot and garlic for five mins until tender and fragrant. Mix in tomatoes, oregano, Italian seasoning, salt, and red flakes and simmer for 6 minutes. Cut the eggplants lengthwise into 1,5-inch slices and season with salt. Grill them for 2-3 minutes per side until softened.

2. Place them on a plate and spoon 2 tbsp of ricotta cheese. Wrap them and arrange them on a greased baking dish. Sprinkle over the sauce the mozzarella cheese. Bake for 15-20 minutes until golden-brown and bubbling.

Per serving: Calories: 362kcal; Fat: 16.6g; Carbs: 38.4g; Protein: 19.3g

44. Homemade Vegetable Casserole

Preparation time: 10 minutes
Cooking time: 35 minutes
Servings: 4
Ingredients:

1 lb. diced and steamed potatoes

2 red bell peppers, halved

1 lb. mushrooms, sliced

2 tomatoes, diced

8 garlic cloves, peeled

1 eggplant, sliced

1 yellow onion, quartered

4 tbsp olive oil

½ tsp dried oregano

¼ tsp caraway seeds

Salt, as required

Directions:

1. Warm up the oven to 390F. In a bowl, mix the bell peppers, mushrooms, tomatoes, eggplant, onion, garlic, salt, olive oil, oregano, and caraway seeds. Set aside.

2. Pour the potatoes on a baking dish and bake for 15 minutes. Top with the veggies mixture and bake for another 15-20 minutes until tender. Serve hot.

Per serving: Calories: 302kcal; Fat: 15g; Carbs: 39.9g; Protein: 8.5g

45. Vegetarian Casserole

Preparation time: 10 minutes
Cooking time: 40 minutes
Servings: 4
Ingredients:

1 onion, finely chopped

1 teaspoon smoked paprika

1 tablespoon rapeseed oil

2 garlic cloves, minced

½ teaspoon ground cumin

2 medium carrots, sliced

1 red pepper, chopped

(14-ounce) cans tomatoes

4 zucchinis, thickly sliced

1¼ cups lentils, cooked

1 tablespoon dried thyme

3 medium sticks celery, finely sliced

1 yellow pepper, chopped

1 vegetable stock cube

4 sprigs fresh thyme

Directions:

1. Heat the rapeseed oil in a heavy-large pan and add the onions.

2. Sauté for about 10 minutes and add the ground cumin, dried thyme, garlic cloves, celery sticks, red pepper, smoked paprika, , carrots and yellow pepper.

40

3. Cook for about 5 min and then stir in the vegetable stock, tomatoes, zucchinis, and fresh thyme.

4. Cook for about 25 minutes and then add the cooked lentils.

5. Let the mixture come to a simmer, and then remove from the heat to serve.

Per serving: Calories: 340kcal; Fat: 5.1g; Carbs: 62.7g; Protein: 19.5g

CHAPTER 4
SEAFOOD

46. Lemon Grilled Shrimp

Preparation time: 4 minutes
Cooking time: 6 minutes
Servings: 4
Ingredients:

2 tablespoons garlic, minced

2 tablespoons fresh Italian parsley, finely chopped

¼ cup extra-virgin olive oil

½ cup lemon juice

1 teaspoon salt

2 pounds jumbo shrimp (21 to 25), peeled and deveined

Special Equipment:

wooden skewers, placed to soak in water for at least 30 minutes

Directions:
1. Whisk the garlic, parsley, olive oil, lemon juice, and salt in a large bowl. Add the shrimp and toss well, making sure the shrimp are coated in the marinade. Set aside to sit for 15 minutes.
2. When ready, skewer the shrimps by piercing through the center. You can place about 5 to 6 shrimps on each skewer.
3. Warm up the grill to high flame. Grill the shrimp for 4 minutes, flipping the shrimp halfway through, or until the shrimp are opaque in the center and pink color on the outside. Serve hot.

Per serving: Calories: 401kcal; Fat: 17.8g; Carbs: 3.9g; Protein: 56.9g

47. Glazed Broiled Salmon

Preparation time: 5 minutes
Cooking time: 5 to 10 minutes
Servings: 4
Ingredients:

(4-ounce / 113-g) salmon fillets

2 tablespoons miso paste

two tbsps. raw honey

one teaspoon coconut aminos

one tsp. rice vinegar

Directions:
1. Preheat the broiler to High. Line a pan with aluminum and add the salmon fillets.
2. Whisk together the miso paste, honey, coconut aminos, and vinegar in a small container. Pour the glaze across the fillets and disperse it uniformly with a brush.
3. Broil for about 5 minutes, or 'til the salmon is browned on top and opaque.
4. Brush any remaining glaze over the salmon and broil for an additional 5 minutes if needed.
5. The cooking time depends on the thickness of the salmon. Let the salmon cool for 5 minutes prior to serving.

Per serving: Calories: 263kcal; Fat: 8.9g; Carbs: 12.8g; Protein: 30.2g

48. Rosemary Trout with Roasted Beets

Preparation time: ten mins
Cooking time: 35 mins
Servings: four
Ingredients:

3 tbsps. olive oil

4 trout fillets, boneless

1 lb. medium beets, peeled and sliced

Salt and black pepper to taste

1 tbsp rosemary, chopped

2 spring onions, chopped

2 tbsp lemon juice

½ cup vegetable stock

Directions:
1. Put in a preheated 390 degree oven.
2. Prepare a parchment-lined baking sheet. Arrange the beets on the sheet, season with salt and pepper, and drizzle with some olive oil. Roast for 20 minutes.
3. Warm the other olive oil inside a griddle across moderate flame.
4. Cook trout fillets for 8 mins on every end; reserve.

5. Include spring onions to the skillet and fry for two mins. Mix in lemon juice and vegetable stock and cook for 5-6 minutes until the sauce thickens.

6. Remove the beets to a plate and top with trout fillets. Pour the sauce all over and sprinkle with rosemary to serve.

Per serving: Calories: 240kcal; Fat: 6g; Carbs: 22g; Protein: 18g

49. Lemon-Parsley Swordfish

Preparation time: 10 minutes
Cooking time: 20 minutes
Servings: 4
Ingredients:

1 cup fresh Italian parsley

¼ cup lemon juice

¼ cup extra-virgin olive oil

¼ cup fresh thyme

2 cloves garlic

½ teaspoon salt

4 swordfish steaks

Olive oil spray

Directions:

1. Warm up the microwave to 450F. Oil a large pot with olive oil spray.

2. Put the parsley, lemon juice, olive oil, thyme, garlic, & salt in a food processor then pulse until smoothly blended.

3. Arrange the swordfish steaks in the greased baking dish and spoon the parsley mixture over the top.

4. Bake for 18 minutes until flaky. Serve the fish among four plates and serve hot.

Per serving: Calories: 396kcal; Fat: 21.7g; Carbs: 2.9g; Protein: 44.2g

50. Hot and Fresh Fishy Steaks

Preparation time: 14 mins
Cooking time: 14 mins
Servings: 2
Ingredients:

one clove, minced garlic

one tbsp lemon juice

one tablespoon brown sugar

1-pound halibut steak

Salt and pepper, as required

quarter teaspoon soy sauce

one teaspoon butter

two tbsps. Greek yogurt

Directions:

1. Over a medium flame, preheat the grill.

2. Mix the butter, sugar, yogurt, lemon juice, soy sauce and seasonings in a bowl.

3. Warm the mixture in a pan.

4. Use this mixture to brush onto the steak while cooking on the griller.

5. Serve hot.

Per serving: Calories: 412kcal; Fat: 19.4g; Carbs: 35.6g; Protein: 25.7g

51. Pesto Fish Fillet

Preparation time: 10 minutes
Cooking time: 8 minutes
Servings: 4
Ingredients:

4 halibut fillets

1/2 cup water

1 tbsp lemon zest, grated

1 tbsp capers

1/2 cup basil, chopped

1 tbsp garlic, chopped

1 avocado, peeled and chopped

Salt and black pepper to taste

Directions:

1. Add lemon zest, capers, basil, garlic, avocado, pepper, and salt into the blender blend until smooth. Place fish fillets on aluminum foil and spread a blended mixture on fish fillets. Fold foil around the fish fillets. Pour water into the pot and place the trivet in the pot. Place foil fish packet on the trivet.

2. Cover skillet with lid and cook on high for 8 minutes. Once done, remove lid. Serve and relish.

Per serving: Calories: 426kcal; Fat: 16.6g; Carbs: 5.5g; Protein: 61.8g

52. Shrimp and Dill Mix

Preparation time: 10 minutes

Cooking time: 10 minutes

Servings: 4

Ingredients:

1-pound shrimp, cooked, peeled and deveined

½ cup raisins

1 cup spring onion, chopped

two tbsps. olive oil

2 tablespoons capers, sliced

two tbsps. dill, sliced

Salt and black pepper to the taste

Directions:

1. Put the oil in a pan and heat it over medium heat, add the onions and raisins and sauté for 2-3 minutes.

2. Add the shrimp and the rest of the ingredients, toss, cook for 6 minutes more, divide into plates and serve with a side salad.

Per serving: Calories: 218kcal; Fat: 12.8g; Carbs: 22.2g; Protein: 4.8g

53. Salmon and Mango Mix

Preparation time: 10 minutes

Cooking time: 25 minutes

Servings: 2

Ingredients:

2 salmon fillets, skinless and boneless

Salt and pepper to the taste

2 tablespoons olive oil

2 garlic cloves, minced

2 mangos, peeled and cubed

1 red chili, chopped

1 small piece ginger, grated

Juice of 1 lime

1 tablespoon cilantro, chopped

Directions:

1. In a roasting pot, mix the salmon with the oil, garlic and the rest of the components except the cilantro; whisk, preheat the microwave at 350 °F and bake for 25 mins.

2. Split everything among plates and serve with the cilantro sprinkled on top.

Per serving: Calories: 251kcal; Fat: 15.9g; Carbs: 26.4g; Protein: 12.4g

54. Salmon and Watermelon Gazpacho

Preparation time: 4 hours

Cooking time: 0 minutes

Servings: 4

Ingredients:

¼ cup basil, chopped

1-pound tomatoes, cubed

1-pound watermelon, cubed

¼ cup red wine vinegar

1/3 cup avocado oil

2 garlic cloves, minced

1 cup smoked salmon, skinless, boneless and cubed

A pinch of salt and black pepper

Directions:

1. In your blender, combine the basil with the watermelon and the rest of the ingredients except the salmon, pulse well and divide into containers.

2. Season every serving with the salmon and serve cold.

Per serving: Calories: 252kcal; Fat: 16.5g; Carbs: 24.8g; Protein: 15.5g

55. Crispy Herb Crusted Halibut

Preparation time: 10 minutes
Cooking time: 20 minutes
Servings: 4
Ingredients:

(5-ounce / 142-g) halibut fillets patted dry

Extra-virgin olive oil for brushing

½ cup coarsely ground unsalted pistachios

1 tablespoon chopped fresh parsley

1 teaspoon chopped fresh basil

1 teaspoon chopped fresh thyme

Pinch sea salt

Pinch freshly ground black pepper

Directions:

1. Preheat the oven to 350F. Prepare a parchment-lined baking sheet.
2. Place the fillets on the pan and brush them generously with olive oil.
3. Stir together the pistachios, parsley, basil, thyme, salt, and pepper in a small bowl. Spoon the nut mixture evenly on the fish, spreading it out so the tops of the fillets are covered.
4. Bake in the preheated oven until it flakes when pressed with a fork, about 20 minutes.
5. Serve instantly.

Per serving: Calories: 262kcal; Fat: 11.0g; Carbs: 4.0g; Protein: 32.0g

56. Tomato Tilapia with Parsley

Preparation time: ten mins
Cooking time: ten mins
Servings: four
Ingredients:

two tbsps. olive oil

4 tilapia fillets, boneless

½ cup tomato sauce

2 tbsp parsley, chopped

Salt and black pepper, as required
Directions:

1. Heat olive oil inside a griddle across moderate flame. Sprinkle tilapia with salt and pepper and cook until golden brown, flipping once for about 6 minutes.
2. Put in the tomato sauce and parsley and cook for an additional 4 minutes.
3. Serve instantly.

Per serving: Calories: 308kcal; Fat: 17g; Carbs: 3g; Protein: 16g

57. Salmon and Green Beans

Preparation time: 10 minutes
Cooking time: 15 minutes
Servings: 4
Ingredients:

3 tablespoons balsamic vinegar

2 tablespoons olive oil

1 garlic clove, minced

½ teaspoons red pepper flakes, crushed

½ teaspoon lime zest, grated

1 and ½ pounds green beans, chopped

Salt and black pepper to the taste

1 red onion, sliced

4 salmon fillets, boneless
Directions:

1. Warm a pot using half of the olive oil, include the vinegar, onion, garlic and the remaining components except the salmon, whisk, cook for six mins and split among plates.
2. Heat the same pan with the rest of the oil over medium-high heat, add the salmon, pepper and salt, cook for 5 minutes on each side, add next to the green beans and serve.

Per serving: Calories: 224kcal; Fat: 15.5g; Carbs: 22.7g; Protein: 16.3g

58. Mediterranean Fish Fillets

Preparation time: 10 minutes

Cooking time: 3 minutes

Servings: 4

Ingredients:

4 cod fillets

1 lb. grape tomatoes, halved

1 cup olives, pitted and sliced

2 tbsp capers

1 tsp dried thyme

two tbsps. olive oil

one teaspoon garlic, crushed

Salt and Black pepper, as required

Directions:

1. Pour 2 cup of water in a pot, then place the steamer rack in the pot. Spray heat-safe baking dish with cooking spray. Add half grape tomatoes into the dish and season with pepper and salt.
2. Arrange fish fillets on top of cherry tomatoes. Drizzle with oil and season with garlic, thyme, capers, pepper, and salt. Spread olives and remaining grape tomatoes on top of fish fillets. Place dish on top of steamer rack in the pot.
3. Put the cover on the pan, choose manual cooking, and set the heat to high for three mins. At that point, release pressure utilizing fast release. Eliminate cover. Serve, and have fun with it!

Per serving: Calories: 212kcal; Fat: 11.9g; Carbs: 7.1g; Protein: 21.4g

59. Roasted Salmon with Asparagus

Preparation time: 5 mins

Cooking time: fifteen mins

Servings: four

Ingredients:

four salmon fillets, skinless

2 tbsp balsamic vinegar

1 bunch of asparagus, trimmed

two tbsps. olive oil

Salt and black pepper, as required

Directions:

1. Warm up the microwave to 380F. In a roasting pan, arrange the salmon fillets and asparagus spears. Drizzle with olive oil, sprinkle with pepper, salt and balsamic vinegar; roast for 12-15 minutes.
2. Serve hot.

Per serving: Calories: 310kcal; Fat: 16g; Carbs: 19g; Protein: 21g

60. Mediterranean Mussels

Preparation time: 10 minutes

Cooking time: 10 minutes

Servings: 4

Ingredients:

1 white onion, sliced

3 tablespoons olive oil

2 teaspoons fennel seeds

4 garlic cloves, minced

1 teaspoon red pepper, crushed

A pinch of salt and black pepper

1 cup chicken stock

1 tablespoon lemon juice

2 and ½ pounds mussels, scrubbed

½ cup parsley, chopped

½ cup tomatoes, cubed

Directions:

1. Heat a pot using the oil over moderate-high flame, include the onion and the garlic and fry for two mins. Include all the ingredients except the mussels, stir and cook for 3 mins more.
2. Add the mussels, cook everything for additional six mins, split everything into containers and serve.

Per serving: Calories: 276kcal; Fat: 9.8g; Carbs: 6.5g; Protein: 20.5g

CHAPTER 5
POULTRY AND MEAT

61. Grilled Pork Chops

Preparation time: 20 minutes
Cooking time: 10 minutes
Servings: 4
Ingredients:

¼ cup extra-virgin olive oil

2 tablespoons fresh thyme leaves

1 teaspoon smoked paprika

1 teaspoon salt

4 pork loin chops, ½-inch-thick

Directions:

1. In a medium bowl, mix the thyme, paprika, olive oil and salt.
2. Put the pork chops in a plastic zip-top bag or a bowl and coat them with the spice mix. Let them marinate for fifteen mins.
3. Warm up the grill to high flame. Cook the pork chops for 4 min. on every end till cooked thoroughly.
4. Serve heated.

Per serving: Calories: 282kcal; Fat: 23.0g; Carbs: 1.0g; Protein: 21.0g

62. Hot Baked Pork

Preparation time: 10 minutes
Cooking time: 2 hours
Servings: 6
Ingredients:

2 lb. pork shoulder

1 onion, chopped

2 tbsp garlic, minced

1 tbsp hot paprika

1 tbsp basil, chopped

3 tbsp olive oil

1 cup chicken broth

Salt and black pepper to taste

Directions:

1. Preheat oven to 350F. Heat oil in a skillet and broil the pork on all sides for about 8-10 minutes; remove to a baking dish. Add all garlic and onion to the pan and fry for three mins till softened.
2. Mix in hot paprika, salt, and pepper for one min and pour in chicken broth. Transfer to the tray, cover with aluminum foil and bake for 90 min. Remove the foil and baking for another 20 minutes until browned on top.
3. Let the pork cool for a few minutes, slice, and sprinkle with basil. Serve beaten with the cooking juices.

Per serving: Calories: 310kcal; Fat: 15g; Carbs: 21g; Protein: 18g

63. Grilled Chicken Breasts with Spinach Pesto

Preparation time: 10 minutes
Cooking time: 15 minutes
Servings: 4
Ingredients:

4 boneless, skinless chicken breasts

¼ cup + 1 tbsp olive oil

1 cup spinach

¼ cup grated Pecorino cheese

Salt and black pepper to taste

¼ cup pine nuts

one garlic clove, crushed

Directions:

1. Rub chicken using salt and black pepper. Grease a grill pot with one tablespoon of olive oil and place across moderate flame. Flip the chicken over after 8-10 minutes on

the grill. Mix spinach, garlic, Pecorino cheese, and pine nuts in a food processor.

2. Slowly, pour in the remaining oil; pulse until smooth. Spoon 1 tbsp of pesto on each breast and cook for an additional 5 minutes.

Per serving: Calories: 493kcal; Fat: 27g; Carbs: 4g; Protein: 53g

64. Saucy Pork with Carrots

Preparation time: ten mins
Cooking time: 40 mins
Servings: four
Ingredients:

one lb. pork loin, sliced

3 garlic cloves, sliced

two tbsps. olive oil

3 carrots, cut

one red onion, chopped

Salt and black pepper as required

three cups chicken stock

two tbsps. tomato pastes

2 tsps. turmeric powder

1 teaspoon dried oregano

2 tbsp parsley, chopped

Directions:

1. Preheat the oven to 360 F. Warm the olive oil in a pot over medium heat and cook pork, onion, and garlic for 8 minutes. Stir in carrots, salt, pepper, stock, tomato paste, turmeric, and oregano and transfer to a baking dish. Bake for 30 minutes. Serve topped with parsley.

Per serving: Calories: 310kcal; Fat: 25g; Carbs: 24g; Protein: 20g

65. Hot Pork Meatballs

Preparation time: 10 minutes
Cooking time: 20 minutes
Servings: 4
Ingredients:

1 lb. ground pork

3 tbsp olive oil

2 tbsp parsley, chopped

2 green onions, chopped

four garlic cloves, crushed

one red chili, sliced

one cup veggie stock

two tbsps. hot paprika

Directions:

1. Combine pork, parsley, green onions, garlic, and red chili in a bowl and form medium balls out of the mixture.

2. Heat olive oil in a griddle across moderate flame. Sear meatballs for 8 minutes on all sides.

3. Stir in stock and hot paprika and simmer for another 12 minutes. Serve hot.

Per serving: Calories: 240kcal; Fat: 19g; Carbs: 12g; Protein: 15g

66. Nut Turkey with Herbs

Preparation time: 10 minutes
Cooking time: 40 minutes
Servings: 4
Ingredients:

1 lb. turkey breast, cubed

½ cup pistachios, toasted and chopped

one tablespoon olive oil

one cup chicken stock

one tablespoon basil, chopped

one tablespoon rosemary, sliced

one tbsp oregano, sliced

one tablespoon parsley, sliced

one tablespoon tarragon, sliced

3 garlic cloves, crushed

three cups tomatoes, chopped

Directions:

1. Warm the olive oil in a skillet over medium heat and cook turkey and garlic for 5 minutes. Stir in stock, basil, rosemary, oregano, parsley, tarragon, almonds, and tomatoes and bring to a simmer.

2. Cook for 35 mins. Serve instantly.

Per serving: Calories: 310kcal; Fat: 12g; Carbs: 20g; Protein: 25g

---

67. Easy Pork Chops in Tomato Sauce

Preparation time: ten mins
Cooking time: ten mins
Servings: four
Ingredients:

two tbsps. olive oil

4 pork loin chops, boneless

6 tomatoes, peeled and crushed

3 tbsp basil, chopped

¼ cup black olives eroded & shared

one yellow onion, sliced

1 garlic clove, minced

Directions:

1. Warm the olive oil in a skillet over medium heat and brown pork chops for 6 minutes on all sides. Share into plates.
2. In the same skillet, stir tomatoes, basil, olives, onion, and garlic and simmer for 4 minutes. Drizzle tomato sauce across pork to serve.

Per serving: Calories: 340kcal; Fat: 18g; Carbs: 13g; Protein: 35g

---

68. Lamb & Vegetable Gratin

Preparation time: 10 mins
Cooking time: 35 mins
Servings: 4
Ingredients:

3 tbsps. olive oil

one lb. lamb chops

½ cup basil leaves, sliced

½ cup mint leaves, chopped

1 tbsp rosemary, chopped

2 garlic cloves, minced

1 eggplant, cubed

2 zucchinis, cubed

1 yellow bell pepper, roughly chopped

2 oz mozzarella cheese, crumbled

8 oz cherry tomatoes, halved

Directions:

1. Warm up the microwave to 380 F. Put lamb chops, basil, mint, rosemary, garlic, olive oil, eggplant, zucchinis, bell pepper, and tomatoes in a roasting pan and bake covered with foil for 27 minutes.
2. Open, spread with mozzarella cheese and bake for another 5-10 minutes until the cheese melts. Serve instantly.

Per serving: Calories: 330kcal; Fat: 17g; Carbs: 20g; Protein: 23g

---

69. Lamb with Green Vegetables

Preparation time: 10 minutes
Cooking time: 60 minutes
Servings: 2
Ingredients:

½ pound green beans, trimmed

½ pound asparagus spears, trimmed

½ cup frozen peas, thawed

2 tomatoes, chopped

1-pound lamb chops

one tablespoon tomato paste

one onion, chopped

2 tbsps. olive oil, divided

Salt and black pepper to taste

Directions:

1. Warm one tbsp oil in a saucepan over medium heat. Sprinkle the chops with salt and pepper. Place in the pan and brown for 8 minutes in total; set aside.
2. In the same pan, sauté onion for 2 minutes until soft.
3. In a bowl, stir the tomato paste and 1 cup of water and pour in the saucepan. Boil and scrape any bits from the bottom.
4. Add the chops back and boil. Simmer at a low heat for 40 minutes. Add in green beans, asparagus, peas, tomatoes, salt, and pepper and cook for 10 minutes until the greens are soft. Serve warm.

Per serving: Calories: 341kcal; Fat: 15.7g; Carbs: 14.8g; Protein: 36.2g

70. Chili Beef with Zucchini

Preparation time: ten mins
Cooking time: 12 mins
Servings: 4
Ingredients:

2 tbsps. olive oil

one lb. beef steaks, cut

2 zucchinis, spiralized

½ cup sweet chili sauce

1 cup carrot, grated

3 tbsp water

1 tbsp chives, chopped

Salt and black pepper to taste

Directions:

1. Warm the olive oil in a skillet over medium heat and brown beef steaks for 8 minutes on both sides; set aside and cover with foil to keep warm. Stir zucchini noodles, chili sauce, carrot, water, salt, and pepper and cook for an additional 3-4 minutes.

2. Remove the foil from the steaks and pour the zucchini mix over to serve.

Per serving: Calories: 360kcal; Fat: 12g; Carbs: 26g; Protein: 37g

71. Spiced Chicken Meatballs

Preparation time: 10 minutes

Cooking time: 20 minutes
Servings: 4
Ingredients:

1-pound chicken meat, ground

1 tablespoon pine nuts, toasted and chopped

1 egg, whisked

2 teaspoons turmeric powder

2 garlic cloves, minced

Salt and black pepper as required

one and ¼ cups heavy cream

two tablespoons olive oil

¼ cup parsley, chopped

one tablespoon chives, chopped

Directions:

1. In a bowl, combine the pine nuts with the chicken and the rest of the ingredients except the oil and the cream; stir well and shape medium meatballs out of this mix.

2. Heat a pan with the oil over medium-high heat, add the meatballs and cook them for 4 minutes on each side.

3. After adding the cream, give all a gentle stir and continue to simmer it across moderate flame for another ten mins. After that, split the mixture among dishes and serve.

Per serving: Calories: 283kcal; Fat: 9.2g; Carbs: 24.4g; Protein: 34.5g

72. Greek-Style Lamb Burgers

Preparation time: ten mins
Cooking time: 10 mins
Servings: four
Ingredients:

one pound (454 gram) ground lamb

½ teaspoon salt

½ teaspoon freshly ground black pepper

2 tablespoons crumbled feta cheese

Buns, toppings, and tzatziki, for serving (optional)

Directions:

1. Preheat the grill to high heat. In a wide bowl, using your hands, stir the lamb with salt and pepper.
2. Divide the meat into 4 portions. Divide each portion in half to make a top and a bottom. Flatten each half into a 3-inch circle.
3. Make a dent in the center of one of the halves and place 1 tablespoon of the feta cheese in the center.
4. Place the second half of the patty on top of the feta cheese and press down to close the 2 halves together, making it resemble a round burger.
5. Grill each side for 3 minutes, for medium-well.
6. Serve on a bun with your favorite toppings and tzatziki sauce, if anticipated.

Per serving: Calories: 345kcal; Fat: 29.0g; Carbs: 1.0g; Protein: 20.0g

73. Mustard Pork Tenderloin

Preparation time: 10 minutes
Cooking time: 25 minutes
Servings: 4
Ingredients:

1 (1½-pound) pork tenderloin

2 garlic cloves, minced

½ cup fresh parsley, chopped

1 tbsp fresh rosemary, chopped

1 tbsp fresh tarragon, chopped

3 tbsp stone-ground mustard

½ tsp cumin powder

½ chili pepper, minced

two tbsps. olive oil

Salt and black pepper, as required

Directions:

1. Warm up microwave to 400 F. In a food processor, blend parsley, tarragon, rosemary, mustard, olive oil, chili pepper, cumin, salt, garlic, and pepper until smooth.

Sprinkle the compote all over the pork and transfer it onto a lined baking tray.
2. Bake in the microwave for 20-25 minutes. Let sit for a few minutes.
3. Slice and serve.

Per serving: Calories: 970kcal; Fat: 29.6g; Carbs: 2.6g; Protein: 163.7g

74. Garlicky Roasted Chicken Drumsticks

Preparation time: ten mins
Cooking time: 60 mins
Servings: four
Ingredients:

1 pound chicken drumsticks

two garlic cloves, minced

one tablespoon butter, softened

one teaspoon paprika

1 lemon, zested

1 tbsp chopped fresh thyme

1 tbsp chopped fresh rosemary

Salt and black pepper to taste

Directions:

1. Preheat oven to 350 F. Mix butter, thyme, paprika, salt, garlic, pepper, and lemon zest in a bowl. Rub the mixture all over the chicken drumsticks and arrange them on a baking dish. Add in ½ cup of water and roast in the oven for 50-60 minutes.
2. Take the chicken out and let it rest for 10 minutes, wrapped in foil. Serve.

Per serving: Calories: 219kcal; Fat: 9.4g; Carbs: 0.5g; Protein: 31.3g

75. Citrus Turkey with Almonds

Preparation time: 10 minutes
Cooking time: 30 minutes
Servings: 4
Ingredients:

¼ cup almonds, chopped

1 lb. turkey breast, sliced

Salt and black pepper, as required

two tbsps. canola oil

1 lemon, juiced and zested

one grapefruit, juiced

1 tbsp rosemary, chopped

3 garlic cloves, minced

1 cup chicken stock

Directions:

1. Heat the olive oil inside a skillet across moderate flame and cook garlic and turkey for 8 mins on both sides. Mix in salt, pepper, lemon juice, lemon zest, grapefruit juice, rosemary, almonds, and stock and bring to a boil.

2. Cook for 20 mins. Serve.

Per serving: Calories: 320kcal; Fat: 13g; Carbs: 19g; Protein: 25g

CHAPTER 6
SIDES AND ACCOMPANIMENTS

76. Pepper & Tomato Dip

Preparation time: 10 mins
Cooking time: 0 mins
Servings: 4
Ingredients:

3 tbsps. olive oil

one cup roasted red peppers, sliced

one lb. tomatoes, peeled and chopped

Salt and black pepper to taste

1 ½ tsp balsamic vinegar

½ tsp oregano, chopped

2 garlic cloves, minced

2 tbsp parsley, chopped

Directions:

1. In a food processor, blend tomatoes, red peppers, salt, pepper, vinegar, oregano, olive oil, garlic, and parsley until smooth.
2. Serve and relish!

Per serving: Calories: 130kcal; Fat: 5g; Carbs: 4g; Protein: 4g

77. Garlic Lentil Dip

Preparation time: 10 mins
Cooking time: fifteen mins
Servings: 6
Ingredients:

3 tbsps. olive oil

one garlic clove, minced

1 cup split red lentils, rinsed

½ tsp dried thyme

1 tbsp balsamic vinegar

Salt and black pepper to taste

Directions:

1. Raise to a boil salted water in a pot across moderate flame. Include in the lentils and cook for 15 mins till cooked through.
2. Drain and put away to cool. Place the lentils, garlic, thyme, vinegar, salt, and pepper in a food processor.
3. Gradually add olive oil while blending 'til smooth. Serve with crackers.

Per serving: Calories: 295kcal; Fat: 10g; Carbs: 16g; Protein: 10g

78. Spanish-Style Avocado Dip

Preparation time: 5 minutes
Cooking time: 0 minutes
Servings: 4
Ingredients:

2 avocados, chopped

½ cup heavy cream

1 serrano pepper, chopped

Salt and black pepper, as required

two tbsps. cilantro, sliced

¼ cup lime juice

Directions:

1. Inside a food processor, blitz heavy cream, serrano pepper, salt, pepper, avocados, cilantro, and lime juice until smooth.
2. Refrigerate prior to serving.

Per serving: Calories: 201kcal; Fat: 15g; Carbs: 8g; Protein: 8g

79. Greek Cucumber Salad

Preparation time: 10 minutes
Cooking time: 0 minutes
Servings: 4
Ingredients:

1 English cucumber

1 cup grape tomatoes halved

1 medium-sized red onion sliced

one teaspoon lemon juice

one tsp olive oil

one-eighth teaspoon dried oregano

one-eighth teaspoon fresh or dried dill

Salt and pepper, as required

Directions:

1. To remove the seeds from a cucumber, cut it in half lengthwise and scoop them out.
2. Halve your tomatoes
3. Make red onion slice
4. Toss together the vegetables and all other ingredients in a bowl, taste, and season to taste.
5. Store in a refrigerator for 2-3 days in an airtight container.

Per serving: Calories: 103kcal; Fat: 1g; Carbs: 6g; Protein: 1g

80. Broccoli with Caramelized Onions & Pine Nuts

Preparation time: ten mins
Cooking time: 25 mins
Servings: 4
Ingredients:

three tbsps. pine nuts with chopped slivered almonds

2 tsp olive oil extra-virgin

1 cup chopped onion

¼ tsp salt

4 cups of broccoli florets

two tsps. balsamic vinegar

1 Freshly ground pepper, as required

Directions:

1. Toast pine nuts (or almonds) over moderate-low flame in a medium-dry griddle, continually mixing for (2 - 3) minutes, until lightly browned and fragrant. To cool, transfer it to a small bowl.
2. In the pan, add oil and heat over medium heat. Add the onion and salt; cook for 15 to 20 minutes, occasionally stirring, adjusting the heat as needed, until soft and golden brown.
3. Meanwhile, steam the broccoli for 4 to 6 minutes, until just tender. Put in a large basin. Stir in the nuts, onion, pepper, and vinegar.
4. Immediately serve.

Per serving: Calories: 102kcal; Fat: 6.9g; Carbs: 9g; Protein: 3.4g

81. Lemon and Garlic with Shredded Green Cabbage

Preparation time: fifteen mins
Cooking time: 0 mins
Servings: 8
Ingredients:

1 garlic clove

two tbsps. freshly squeezed lemon juice

two tbsps. additional-virgin olive oil

one lb. chopped green cabbage with a crunchy core

Kosher salt

Directions:

1. Pound the garlic in a mortar to form a puree. Stir in olive oil and lemon juice.
2. Mix well the cabbage in a bowl with the dressing. Salt to season and toss again. Serve it immediately or lightly chilled.

Per serving: Calories: 308kcal; Fat: 17g; Carbs: 3g; Protein: 16g

82. Pecorino Spinach Frittata

Preparation time: 25 minutes
Cooking time: 10 minutes
Servings: 4
Ingredients:

1 cup spinach, torn into pieces

1 cup Pecorino-Romano cheese, shredded

1/3 cup heavy cream

2 garlic cloves, minced

8 eggs

2 tbsp olive oil

1 onion, chopped

1 tsp Italian seasoning

½ tsp hot paprika

Directions:

1. Preheat oven to 380 F. Heat the olive oil in a skillet over medium heat. Add in the onion and stir-fry for 4 minutes.
2. Stir in Italian seasoning, paprika, and garlic and cook for 1 more minute. In a bowl, whisk the eggs with heavy cream. Add in spinach and mix well.
3. Pour over the onion mixture and bake for 10 minutes until the eggs are set. Sprinkle with Pecorino cheese and continue baking until the cheese melts about 3-5 mins.
4. Allow it to sit for a couple mins prior to chopping. Serve warm.

Per serving: Calories: 258kcal; Fat: 21g; Carbs: 4.6g; Protein: 14.1g

83. Strawberry Spinach Salad with Poppyseed Dressing

Preparation time: ten mins
Cooking time: zero mins
Servings: 4
Ingredients:

one-third cup of olive oil

3 tbsps. juice of lemon or apple cider vinegar

3 tbsp honey

1 tbsp poppy seeds

1 tsp mustard powder (optional)

Salt and pepper to taste

6 cups spinach fresh

1-pint strawberries washed, hulled and sliced

Directions:

1. Add the oil, vinegar, honey, poppy seeds, mustard powder, salt, pepper and whisk together until combined inside a big salad container.
2. Include the spinach and strawberries, then whisk them all together. Immediately serve. Enjoy! Enjoy!

Per serving: Calories: 340kcal; Fat: 16g; Carbs: 23g; Protein: 35g

84. Parmesan Cauliflower Purée

Preparation time: 10 minutes
Cooking time: 10 minutes
Servings: 4
Ingredients:

¼ cup grated Parmesan cheese

4 cups cauliflower florets

¼ cup milk

two tbsps. butter

two tbsps. wholegrain mustard

one teaspoon ground cumin

one teaspoon crushed chilies

Salt and black pepper, as required

Directions:

1. Boil the cauliflower in a large-deep pot of salted water for 10 min. Drain and put in a

large bowl. Include in milk, butter, cheese, olive oil, cumin, salt, and pepper. Mash until smooth with a potato masher.

2. Top with crushed chilies and serve.

Per serving: Calories: 117kcal; Fat: 8.2g; Carbs: 8.3g; Protein: 4.6g

85. Easy Mediterranean Orange and Pomegranate

Preparation time: 20 mins
Cooking time: zero mins
Servings: 6
Ingredients:

one and a half oz. thinly sliced of red onions

25 fresh chopped mint leaves

6 navels cut into rounds oranges

Pinch kosher salt

Pinch sweet paprika

Pinch ground cinnamon

Seeds arils of 1 pomegranate

Dressing:

1 lime juice

1 tbsp extra virgin olive oil

1 tbsp honey

1 ½ tsp orange blossom water

Directions:

1. Get the dressing done. Lime juice, olives oil, honey and orange blossom water are mixed in a small bowl. Just set aside.

2. Lay the sliced onions in a container of ice-cold water. Set aside for five to ten mins and then remove the onions from the water and dry thoroughly.

3. Have prepared a serving dish. Pour half the amount of chopped mint leaves onto the plate, then arrange the orange slices and onions on top. Sprinkle some salt, sweet paprika, and cinnamon with the mixture. Spread the pomegranate seeds on top of them now.

4. Drizzle the dressing over the orange pomegranate salad or spoon it over (You can add a little if you want of the dressing.)

5. Finally, add the remaining fresh mint leaves to the salad. Set aside before serving for 5 minutes or so.

Per serving: Calories: 276kcal; Fat: 9.8g; Carbs: 6.5g; Protein: 20.5g

86. Truffle Popcorn

Preparation time: 20 minutes
Cooking time: 20 minutes
Servings: 6
Ingredients:

2 tbsp butter, melted

1 tbsp truffle oil

8 cups air-popped popcorn

2 tbsp packed brown sugar

2 tbsp Italian seasoning

¼ tsp sea salt

Directions:

1. Preheat oven to 350 F. Combine butter, Italian seasoning, brown sugar, and salt in a bowl. Pour the popcorn and stir well to coat.

2. Remove to a baking dish and bake for 15 minutes, stirring frequently. Drizzle with truffle oil and serve.

Per serving: Calories: 80kcal; Fat: 5g; Carbs: 8.4g; Protein: 1.1g

87. Calamari in Cilantro Sauce

Preparation time: ten mins
Cooking time: 15 mins
Servings: four
Ingredients:

two tbsps. olive oil

2 lb. calamari, sliced into rings

four garlic cloves, crushed

one lime, juiced

two tbsps. balsamic vinegar

three tbsps. cilantro, sliced

Directions:

1. Warm the olive oil in a griddle across moderate flame and sauté garlic, lime juice, balsamic vinegar, and cilantro for 5 minutes.

2. Stir in calamari rings and cook for another 10 minutes. Serve warm.

Per serving: Calories: 290kcal; Fat: 19g; Carbs: 10g; Protein: 19g

88. Turkish Beets & Leeks with Creamy Yogurt Sauce

Preparation time: 10 minutes
Cooking time: 30 minutes
Servings: 4
Ingredients:

½ lb. leeks, thickly sliced

1 lb. red beets, sliced

1 cup yogurt

2 garlic cloves, finely minced

¼ tsp cumin, ground

¼ tsp dried parsley

¼ cup fresh parsley, to garnish

5 tbsp olive oil

1 tsp dill

Salt and black pepper to taste

Directions:

1. Preheat the oven to 390 F. Arrange the beets and leeks on a greased roasting dish. Sprinkle with some olive oil, cumin, dried parsley, black pepper, and salt. Bake in the oven for 25-30 minutes. Transfer to a serving platter. In a bowl, stir in dill, garlic, yogurt and the remaining olive oil. Whisk to combine.
2. Drizzle the veggies with the yogurt sauce and season using fresh parsley to serve.

Per serving: Calories: 281kcal; Fat: 18.7g; Carbs: 24.2g; Protein: 6.4g

89. Cucumber Bites

Preparation time: 5 minutes
Cooking time: 0 minutes
Servings: 4
Ingredients:

2 tbsp olive oil

2 cucumbers, sliced into rounds

1 cup cherry tomatoes, halved

Salt and black pepper to taste

1 red chili pepper, dried

8 oz cream cheese, softened

1 tbsp balsamic vinegar

1 tsp chives, chopped

Directions:

1. Inside a container, combine cream cheese, balsamic vinegar, olive oil, and chives.
2. Spread the mixture over the cucumber rounds and top with the cherry tomato halves. Serve.

Per serving: Calories: 130kcal; Fat: 3g; Carbs: 7g; Protein: 3g

90. Baked Apples with Cardamom Sauce

Preparation time: ten mins
Cooking time: twenty mins
Servings: 2
Ingredients:

one and a half tsp cardamom

one tsp olive oil

½ tsp salt

4 firm apples, peeled, cored, and sliced

2 tbsp honey

2 tbsp milk

Directions:

1. Preheat oven to 390 deg. F. In a bowl, combine apple slices, salt and half tsp of the cardamom. Place them on a greased pan dish and cook for 20 mins. Eradicate to a serving plate. In the meantime, place milk, honey, and remaining cardamom in a pot over medium heat.

2. Cook until simmer. Drop the sauce across the apples and serve immediately.

Per serving: Calories: 287kcal; Fat: 3g; Carbs: 69g; Protein: 2g

CHAPTER 7
DESSERTS

91. Raspberries & Lime Frozen Yogurt

Preparation time: ten mins
Cooking time: zero mins
Servings: four
Ingredients:

2 cups fresh raspberries

4 cups vanilla frozen yogurt

one lime, zested

¼ cup chopped praline pecans
Directions:
1. Divide the frozen yogurt into 4 dessert glasses. Top with raspberries, lime zest, and pecans. Serve immediately.

Per serving: Calories: 142kcal; Fat: 3.4g; Carbs: 26.2g; Protein: 3.7g

92. Poached Pears with Whipped Cream

Preparation time: 10 minutes
Cooking time: 50 minutes
Servings: 4
Ingredients:

4 Bosc pears, peeled

¼ tsp cardamom seeds

1 cup orange juice

1 cinnamon stick

1-star anise

1 tbsp Cointreau orange liqueur

1 tsp allspice berries

1 tsp orange zest

3 cups red wine

1 cup sugar

1 cup whipping cream to serve
Directions:
1. Place orange liqueur and red wine in a pot over medium heat and bring to a boil. Set the heat to low and add the cardamom seeds, cinnamon stick, allspice berries, orange juice, orange zest, star anise; simmer for 5 minutes. Add the pears and sugar, cover, and poach for about 25-30 min. until tender. Remove the pears and set them aside. Drip

the cooking liquid through a sieve, then return it to the pot.
2. Bring to a boil then cook until the liquid obtains a syrup-like consistency, about 10-15 minutes. Pour the sauce over the pears, top with whipping cream, and serve.

Per serving: Calories: 226kcal; Fat: 4.6g; Carbs: 6.6g; Protein: 11.3g

93. Strawberry Popsicles

Preparation time: ten mins + 4 hours for freezing
Cooking time: 0 mins
Servings: 8
Ingredients:

two and a half cups strawberries

½ cup almond milk
Directions:
1. Wash the strawberries water and remove their hulls.
2. Blend the almond milk and strawberries in a food processor until smooth.
3. Place the mixture into molds with sticks and let them freeze for four hrs.

Per serving: Calories: 56kcal; Fat: 4.6g; Carbs: 3.9g; Protein: 0.7g

94. Honey Berry Granita

Preparation time: 30 minutes
Cooking time: 0 minutes
Servings: 4
Ingredients:

1 tsp lemon juice

¼ cup honey

1 cup fresh strawberries

1 cup fresh raspberries

1 cup fresh blueberries
Directions:
1. Bring 2-cup of water to a boil in a pot over high heat. Stir in honey until dissolved. Remove from the heat and mix in berries and lemon juice; let cool.

2. Once cooled, add the mixture to a food processor and pulse until smooth. Transfer to a shallow glass and freeze for 1 hour. Stir with a fork and freeze for 30 more minutes.

3. Repeat a couple of times. Serve in dessert dishes.

Per serving: Calories: 115kcal; Fat: 1g; Carbs: 29g; Protein: 1g

95. Chocolate-Covered Strawberries

Preparation time: 30 minutes
Cooking time: 0 minutes
Servings: 4
Ingredients:

1 cup chocolate chips

¼ cup coconut flakes

1 lb. strawberries

½ tsp vanilla extract

½ tsp ground nutmeg

¼ tsp salt

Directions:

1. Melt chocolate chips for 30 seconds. Remove and stir in vanilla, nutmeg, and salt. Let cool for 2-3 minutes. Soak strawberries into the chocolate and then into the coconut flakes. Place on a waxed paper-lined cookie sheet and let sit for 30 minutes until the chocolate dries. Serve.

Per serving: Calories: 275kcal; Fat: 20g; Carbs: 21g; Protein: 6g

96. Summertime Fruit Salad

Preparation time: 30 minutes
Cooking time: 0 minutes
Servings: 6
Ingredients:

1-pound strawberries, hulled and sliced thinly

3 medium peaches, sliced thinly

6 ounces blueberries

1 tablespoon fresh mint, chopped

2 tablespoons lemon juice

1 tablespoon honey

2 teaspoons balsamic vinegar

Directions:

1. In a salad bowl, combine all ingredients. Gently toss to coat all ingredients. Chill for 50 minutes prior to serving.

Per serving: Calories: 146kcal; Fat: 3.4g; Carbs: 22.8g; Protein: 8.1g

97. Olive Oil Brownies

Preparation time: 7 minutes
Cooking time: 25 minutes
Servings: 9
Ingredients:

¼ cup olive oil

¼ cup Greek yogurt

¾ cup sugar

1 teaspoon vanilla extract

4 eggs

½ cup flour

⅓ cup cocoa powder

¼ teaspoon baking powder

¼ teaspoon salt

⅓ cup walnuts, chopped

Directions:

1. Preheat the oven to 350F and meanwhile line a pan with parchment paper.

2. Blend the olive oil and sugar in a blender. Add the vanilla extract and mix well.

3. Add the beaten eggs, walnuts, and yogurt and mix well.

4. Blend the flour, cocoa powder, salt, and baking powder in another bowl and add them to the olive oil mixture. Decant the mixture into the baking pan.

5. Set the timer for 25 minutes and bake. Once it has cooled, cut it into squares.

Per serving: Calories: 150kcal; Fat: 8.4g; Carbs: 56.5g; Protein: 54.1g

98. Mediterranean Style Fruit Medley

Preparation time: five mins
Cooking time: zero mins

Servings: 6
Ingredients:

four Fuyu persimmons, sliced into wedges

1 ½ cups grapes, halved

8 mint leaves, chopped

1 tablespoon lemon juice

1 tablespoon honey

½ cups almond, toasted and chopped

Directions:

1. Combine all ingredients in a bowl.
2. Toss, then chill before serving.

Per serving: Calories: 159kcal; Fat: 4g; Carbs: 32g; Protein: 3g

---

99. Strawberry & Cocoa Yogurt

Preparation time: 5 minutes
Cooking time: 0 minutes
Servings: 4
Ingredients:

¾ cup Greek yogurt

1 tbsp cocoa powder

¼ cup strawberries, chopped

5 drops vanilla stevia

Directions:

1. Combine cocoa powder, strawberries, yogurt, and stevia in a bowl. Serve instantly.

Per serving: Calories: 210kcal; Fat: 9g; Carbs: 8g; Protein: 5g

---

100. Maple Grilled Pineapple

Preparation time: 5 minutes
Cooking time: 10 minutes
Servings: 4
Ingredients:

1 tbsp maple syrup

1 pineapple, peeled and cut into wedges

½ tsp ground cinnamon

Directions:

1. Preheat a grill pan over high heat. Drizzle the fruit in a bowl with maple syrup; sprinkle with ground cinnamon.
2. Grill for about 7-8 minutes, occasionally turning until the fruit chars slightly. Serve.

Per serving: Calories: 120kcal; Fat: 1g; Carbs: 33g; Protein: 1g

Conversion Chart

Volume Equivalents (Liquid)

US Standard	US Standard (ounces)	Metric (approximate)
2 tablespoons	1 fl. oz.	30 mL
¼ cup	2 fl. oz.	60 mL
½ cup	4 fl. oz.	120 mL
1 cup	8 fl. oz.	240 mL
1½ cups	12 fl. oz.	355 mL
2 cups or 1 pint	16 fl. oz.	475 mL
4 cups or 1 quart	32 fl. oz.	1 L
1 gallon	128 fl. oz.	4 L

Volume Equivalents (Dry)

US Standard	Metric (approximate)
⅛ teaspoon	0.5 mL
¼ teaspoon	1 mL
½ teaspoon	2 mL
¾ teaspoon	4 mL
1 teaspoon	5 mL
1 tablespoon	15 mL
¼ cup	59 mL
⅓ cup	79 mL
½ cup	118 mL
⅔ cup	156 mL
¾ cup	177 mL
1 cup	235 mL
2 cups or 1 pint	475 mL
3 cups	700 mL
4 cups or 1 quart	1 L

Oven Temperatures

Fahrenheit (F)	Celsius (C) (approximate)
250°F	120°C
300°F	150°C
325°F	165°C
350°F	180°C
375°F	190°C
400°F	200°C
425°F	220°C
450°F	230°C

Weight Equivalents

US Standard	Metric (approximate)
1 tablespoon	15 g
½ ounce	15 g
1 ounce	30 g
2 ounces	60 g
4 ounces	115 g
8 ounces	225 g
12 ounces	340 g
16 ounces or 1 pound	455 g

12 - Weeks Meal Plan

Week 1

Days	Breakfast	Lunch	Dinner	Dessert	Calories (kcal)
1	Artichoke & Bean Spread	Nut Turkey with Herbs	Cauliflower Curry	Chocolate-Covered Strawberries	1108
2	Almond Spinach with Chickpeas	Hot and Fresh Fishy Steaks	Spiced Chicken Meatballs	Strawberry Popsicles	981
3	Cheesy Grilled Asparagus	Mediterranean Cobb Salad	Vegetarian Casserole	Raspberries & Lime Frozen Yogurt	809
4	Garlic Lentil-Walnut Spread with Cilantro	Hot Baked Pork	Lamb & Spinach Soup	Poached Pears with Whipped Cream	1060
5	Jalapeno Poppers Stuffed with Hummus	Zucchini Noodles Marinara	Salmon and Mango Mix	Honey Berry Granita	825
6	Grilled Eggplant Rounds	Lemon Grilled Shrimp	Cheesy Eggplant Rolls	Olive Oil Brownies	784
7	Cream Cheese & Tomato Toast	Mustard Pork Tenderloin	Minestrone Soup	Summertime Fruit Salad	1586

Week 2

Days	Breakfast	Lunch	Dinner	Dessert	Calories (kcal)
1	Parmesan Sandwiches	Loaded Portobello Mushrooms	Crispy Herb Crusted Halibut	Strawberry & Cocoa Yogurt	1269
2	Cheese & Cucumber Mini Sandwiches	Pesto Fish Fillet	Carrot Salad with Lemon Vinaigrette	Mediterranean Style Fruit Medley	997
3	Almond & Parmesan Stuffed Cucumbers	Saucy Pork with Carrots	Roasted Salmon with Asparagus	Maple Grilled Pineapple	922
4	Double Tomato Bruschetta	Eggplant, Arugula & Sweet Potato Mix	Garlicky Roasted Chicken Drumsticks	Chocolate-Covered Strawberries	919
5	Thyme Artichoke with Aioli	Tomato Tilapia with Parsley	Greek-Style Potatoes	Strawberry Popsicles	902
6	Roasted Pepper Hummus	Citrus Turkey with Almonds	Mediterranean Salad Recipe	Raspberries & Lime Frozen Yogurt	943

| 7 | Garbanzo Patties with Yogurt Sauce | Pork Meatball Soup | Glazed Broiled Salmon | Poached Pears with Whipped Cream | 989 |

Week 3

Days	Breakfast	Lunch	Dinner	Dessert	Calories (kcal)
1	Red Pepper and Fresh Mozzarella	Simple Sautéed Cauliflower	Mediterranean Mussels	Honey Berry Granita	753.5
2	Artichoke & Bean Spread	Grilled Chicken Breasts with Spinach Pesto	Catalan-Style Spinach	Olive Oil Brownies	1034
3	Almond Spinach with Chickpeas	Lemon-Parsley Swordfish	Chili Beef with Zucchini	Summertime Fruit Salad	1132
4	Cheesy Grilled Asparagus	Italian Sausage & Seafood Soup	Stuffed Bell Peppers	Strawberry & Cocoa Yogurt	1321
5	Garlic Lentil-Walnut Spread with Cilantro	Lamb & Vegetable Gratin	Spicy Lentil Soup	Mediterranean Style Fruit Medley	1054
6	Jalapeno Poppers Stuffed with Hummus	Brussels Sprouts And Pistachios	Mediterranean Fish Fillets	Maple Grilled Pineapple	708
7	Grilled Eggplant Rounds	Salmon and Green Beans	Corn & Black Bean Salad	Chocolate-Covered Strawberries	933

Week 4

Days	Breakfast	Lunch	Dinner	Dessert	Calories (kcal)
1	Cream Cheese & Tomato Toast	Lamb with Green Vegetables	Cucumber and Tomato Salad	Strawberry Popsicles	677.3
2	Parmesan Sandwiches	Spiralized Carrot with Peas	Hot Pork Meatballs	Raspberries & Lime Frozen Yogurt	1208
3	Cheese & Cucumber Mini Sandwiches	Garlic Kale with Almonds	Shrimp and Dill Mix	Poached Pears with Whipped Cream	757
4	Almond & Parmesan Stuffed Cucumbers	Easy Pork Chops in Tomato Sauce	Chili Artichokes with Carrots	Honey Berry Granita	990
5	Double Tomato Bruschetta	Rosemary Trout with Roasted Beets	Greek-Style Lamb Burgers	Olive Oil Brownies	950
6	Thyme Artichoke with Aioli	Homemade Vegetable Casserole	German Hot Potato Salad	Summertime Fruit Salad	773

| 7 | Roasted Pepper Hummus | Grilled Pork Chops | Salmon and Watermelon Gazpacho | Strawberry & Cocoa Yogurt | 1004 |

Week 5

Days	Breakfast	Lunch	Dinner	Dessert	Calories (kcal)
1	Artichoke & Bean Spread	Nut Turkey with Herbs	Cauliflower Curry	Chocolate-Covered Strawberries	1108
2	Almond Spinach with Chickpeas	Hot and Fresh Fishy Steaks	Spiced Chicken Meatballs	Strawberry Popsicles	981
3	Cheesy Grilled Asparagus	Mediterranean Cobb Salad	Vegetarian Casserole	Raspberries & Lime Frozen Yogurt	809
4	Garlic Lentil-Walnut Spread with Cilantro	Hot Baked Pork	Lamb & Spinach Soup	Poached Pears with Whipped Cream	1060
5	Jalapeno Poppers Stuffed with Hummus	Zucchini Noodles Marinara	Salmon and Mango Mix	Honey Berry Granita	825
6	Grilled Eggplant Rounds	Lemon Grilled Shrimp	Cheesy Eggplant Rolls	Olive Oil Brownies	784
7	Cream Cheese & Tomato Toast	Mustard Pork Tenderloin	Minestrone Soup	Summertime Fruit Salad	1586

Week 6

Days	Breakfast	Lunch	Dinner	Dessert	Calories (kcal)
1	Parmesan Sandwiches	Loaded Portobello Mushrooms	Crispy Herb Crusted Halibut	Strawberry & Cocoa Yogurt	1269
2	Cheese & Cucumber Mini Sandwiches	Pesto Fish Fillet	Carrot Salad with Lemon Vinaigrette	Mediterranean Style Fruit Medley	997
3	Almond & Parmesan Stuffed Cucumbers	Saucy Pork with Carrots	Roasted Salmon with Asparagus	Maple Grilled Pineapple	922
4	Double Tomato Bruschetta	Eggplant, Arugula & Sweet Potato Mix	Garlicky Roasted Chicken Drumsticks	Chocolate-Covered Strawberries	919
5	Thyme Artichoke with Aioli	Tomato Tilapia with Parsley	Greek-Style Potatoes	Strawberry Popsicles	902
6	Roasted Pepper Hummus	Citrus Turkey with Almonds	Mediterranean Salad Recipe	Raspberries & Lime Frozen Yogurt	943

| 7 | Garbanzo Patties with Yogurt Sauce | Pork Meatball Soup | Glazed Broiled Salmon | Poached Pears with Whipped Cream | 989 |

Week 7

Days	Breakfast	Lunch	Dinner	Dessert	Calories (kcal)
1	Red Pepper and Fresh Mozzarella	Simple Sautéed Cauliflower	Mediterranean Mussels	Honey Berry Granita	753.5
2	Artichoke & Bean Spread	Grilled Chicken Breasts with Spinach Pesto	Catalan-Style Spinach	Olive Oil Brownies	1034
3	Almond Spinach with Chickpeas	Lemon-Parsley Swordfish	Chili Beef with Zucchini	Summertime Fruit Salad	1132
4	Cheesy Grilled Asparagus	Italian Sausage & Seafood Soup	Stuffed Bell Peppers	Strawberry & Cocoa Yogurt	1321
5	Garlic Lentil-Walnut Spread with Cilantro	Lamb & Vegetable Gratin	Spicy Lentil Soup	Mediterranean Style Fruit Medley	1054
6	Jalapeno Poppers Stuffed with Hummus	Brussels Sprouts And Pistachios	Mediterranean Fish Fillets	Maple Grilled Pineapple	708
7	Grilled Eggplant Rounds	Salmon and Green Beans	Corn & Black Bean Salad	Chocolate-Covered Strawberries	933

Week 8

Days	Breakfast	Lunch	Dinner	Dessert	Calories (kcal)
1	Cream Cheese & Tomato Toast	Lamb with Green Vegetables	Cucumber and Tomato Salad	Strawberry Popsicles	677.3
2	Parmesan Sandwiches	Spiralized Carrot with Peas	Hot Pork Meatballs	Raspberries & Lime Frozen Yogurt	1208
3	Cheese & Cucumber Mini Sandwiches	Garlic Kale with Almonds	Shrimp and Dill Mix	Poached Pears with Whipped Cream	757
4	Almond & Parmesan Stuffed Cucumbers	Easy Pork Chops in Tomato Sauce	Chili Artichokes with Carrots	Honey Berry Granita	990
5	Double Tomato Bruschetta	Rosemary Trout with Roasted Beets	Greek-Style Lamb Burgers	Olive Oil Brownies	950
6	Thyme Artichoke with Aioli	Homemade Vegetable Casserole	German Hot Potato Salad	Summertime Fruit Salad	773

| 7 | Roasted Pepper Hummus | Grilled Pork Chops | Salmon and Watermelon Gazpacho | Strawberry & Cocoa Yogurt | 1004 |

Week 9

Days	Breakfast	Lunch	Dinner	Dessert	Calories (kcal)
1	Artichoke & Bean Spread	Nut Turkey with Herbs	Cauliflower Curry	Chocolate-Covered Strawberries	1108
2	Almond Spinach with Chickpeas	Hot and Fresh Fishy Steaks	Spiced Chicken Meatballs	Strawberry Popsicles	981
3	Cheesy Grilled Asparagus	Mediterranean Cobb Salad	Vegetarian Casserole	Raspberries & Lime Frozen Yogurt	809
4	Garlic Lentil-Walnut Spread with Cilantro	Hot Baked Pork	Lamb & Spinach Soup	Poached Pears with Whipped Cream	1060
5	Jalapeno Poppers Stuffed with Hummus	Zucchini Noodles Marinara	Salmon and Mango Mix	Honey Berry Granita	825
6	Grilled Eggplant Rounds	Lemon Grilled Shrimp	Cheesy Eggplant Rolls	Olive Oil Brownies	784
7	Cream Cheese & Tomato Toast	Mustard Pork Tenderloin	Minestrone Soup	Summertime Fruit Salad	1586

Week 10

Days	Breakfast	Lunch	Dinner	Dessert	Calories (kcal)
1	Parmesan Sandwiches	Loaded Portobello Mushrooms	Crispy Herb Crusted Halibut	Strawberry & Cocoa Yogurt	1269
2	Cheese & Cucumber Mini Sandwiches	Pesto Fish Fillet	Carrot Salad with Lemon Vinaigrette	Mediterranean Style Fruit Medley	997
3	Almond & Parmesan Stuffed Cucumbers	Saucy Pork with Carrots	Roasted Salmon with Asparagus	Maple Grilled Pineapple	922
4	Double Tomato Bruschetta	Eggplant, Arugula & Sweet Potato Mix	Garlicky Roasted Chicken Drumsticks	Chocolate-Covered Strawberries	919
5	Thyme Artichoke with Aioli	Tomato Tilapia with Parsley	Greek-Style Potatoes	Strawberry Popsicles	902
6	Roasted Pepper Hummus	Citrus Turkey with Almonds	Mediterranean Salad Recipe	Raspberries & Lime Frozen Yogurt	943

7	Garbanzo Patties with Yogurt Sauce	Pork Meatball Soup	Glazed Broiled Salmon	Poached Pears with Whipped Cream	989

Week 11

Days	Breakfast	Lunch	Dinner	Dessert	Calories (kcal)
1	Red Pepper and Fresh Mozzarella	Simple Sautéed Cauliflower	Mediterranean Mussels	Honey Berry Granita	753.5
2	Artichoke & Bean Spread	Grilled Chicken Breasts with Spinach Pesto	Catalan-Style Spinach	Olive Oil Brownies	1034
3	Almond Spinach with Chickpeas	Lemon-Parsley Swordfish	Chili Beef with Zucchini	Summertime Fruit Salad	1132
4	Cheesy Grilled Asparagus	Italian Sausage & Seafood Soup	Stuffed Bell Peppers	Strawberry & Cocoa Yogurt	1321
5	Garlic Lentil-Walnut Spread with Cilantro	Lamb & Vegetable Gratin	Spicy Lentil Soup	Mediterranean Style Fruit Medley	1054
6	Jalapeno Poppers Stuffed with Hummus	Brussels Sprouts And Pistachios	Mediterranean Fish Fillets	Maple Grilled Pineapple	708
7	Grilled Eggplant Rounds	Salmon and Green Beans	Corn & Black Bean Salad	Chocolate-Covered Strawberries	933

Week 12

Days	Breakfast	Lunch	Dinner	Dessert	Calories (kcal)
1	Cream Cheese & Tomato Toast	Lamb with Green Vegetables	Cucumber and Tomato Salad	Strawberry Popsicles	677.3
2	Parmesan Sandwiches	Spiralized Carrot with Peas	Hot Pork Meatballs	Raspberries & Lime Frozen Yogurt	1208
3	Cheese & Cucumber Mini Sandwiches	Garlic Kale with Almonds	Shrimp and Dill Mix	Poached Pears with Whipped Cream	757
4	Almond & Parmesan Stuffed Cucumbers	Easy Pork Chops in Tomato Sauce	Chili Artichokes with Carrots	Honey Berry Granita	990
5	Double Tomato Bruschetta	Rosemary Trout with Roasted Beets	Greek-Style Lamb Burgers	Olive Oil Brownies	950
6	Thyme Artichoke with Aioli	Homemade Vegetable Casserole	German Hot Potato Salad	Summertime Fruit Salad	773

| 7 | Roasted Pepper Hummus | Grilled Pork Chops | Salmon and Watermelon Gazpacho | Strawberry & Cocoa Yogurt | 1004 |

Index

Spicy Lentil Soup; 30
Spiralized Carrot with Peas; 38
Strawberry & Cocoa Yogurt; 66
Strawberry Popsicles; 64
Strawberry Spinach Salad with Poppyseed Dressing;
  59
Stuffed Bell Peppers; 36
Summertime Fruit Salad; 65

Thyme Artichoke with Aioli; 21
Tomato Tilapia with Parsley; 46
Truffle Popcorn; 60
Turkish Beets & Leeks with Creamy Yogurt Sauce; 61
Vegetarian Casserole; 40
Veggie & Chicken Soup; 30
Zucchini Noodles Marinara; 37

Conclusion

The Mediterranean diet isn't only an approach to shed weight. However, it is an approach to transform you completely. It consists of a lot of olive oil, fish, vegetables, dairy products, etc.

Excess weight around the stomach is connected with numerous issues that could have lasting effects. The best cure is to consume and, in the meantime, work out, making it the exceedingly fit way to live. Try the pointers beneath to see the advantages for yourself. While the Mediterranean diet is not generally known to be a perfect diet for weight reduction, it is recognized as a decent eating routine for getting a lean, flat stomach. The Mediterranean diet is a diet filled with numerous supplement-rich natural products.

The Mediterranean diet is not a fad diet, in any case, not at all a weight-loss diet. In any case, it isn't a weight-loss diet, yet rather one that serves the immaculate function of making you feel fit-stated. The initial benefit anyone observes with this program is for the body to be light and unblighted of fat. While a few may lose weight with this regime, this doesn't have anything to do with getting you the skinny body you wish. The full answer to weight reduction is not to limit calorie intake but to cut out stress from the body, in this manner decreasing the body's rest level.

A good word for supplements to the Mediterranean diet that we would normally see is olive oil. The olive oil not only serves as a complement to your nourishment routine. Additionally, it is a cure for your ailments. Olive oil has been prescribed for its outstanding benefits since the old age of Hippocrates, and for a good reason. It may be the best addition for your diet routine by a wide edge over all other alternatives in existence today.

Mediterranean diet points the direction to a long, affable life. The confirmation is there, it won't shock anyone to see that a Mediterranean diet can increase your life expectancy since this kind of sustenance is known to be good for you.

Made in the USA
Las Vegas, NV
08 July 2023